MW01578971

Knowledge Nirvana®

*Achieving the Competitive Advantage
Through Enterprise Content Management
and Optimizing Team Collaboration*

Jüris Kelley

Copyright © 2002 Knowledge in Motion LLC

Knowledge Nirvana® by Jüris Kelley

All rights reserved under international and Pan-American Copyright Conventions.

Printed in the United States of America. No part of this publication may be reproduced or transmitted in any form or by any means without written permission of the publisher.

Library of Congress Control Number: 2002106161
ISBN: 1-591601-08-8

Visit the Knowledge Nirvana website at: KnowledgeNirvana.com

First Edition

Knowledge Nirvana is a registered mark of Jüris Kelley. Other trademarks and servicemarks are the property of their respective owners.

Xulon Press
11350 Random Hills Road
Suite 800
Fairfax, VA 22030
(703) 279-6511
XulonPress.com

To order additional copies, call 1-866-909-BOOK (2665).

知

The Mandarin Character for "Knowledge"

Disclaimer

This book is designed to provide general information on Knowledge Management and related topics. It is sold with the understanding that the book is intended to complement, amplify, and supplement other texts and methodologies. You are urged to read all the other available material and tailor this information to your individual needs. Every effort has been made to make this book as complete and as accurate as possible. However, there may be mistakes, both typographical and in content. Therefore, this text should be used only as a general guide and not as the ultimate source of information. The author and publisher shall have neither liability nor responsibility to any person or entity with respect to any loss or damage caused, or alleged to have been caused, directly or indirectly, by the information contained in this book.

Acknowledgments

There are many people who provided assistance to me while I wrote this book. I am most grateful to Diana Abrials for her invaluable assistance in editing (hey, classics majors are really useful); Bill Bivens for his analysis, commentary, and wisdom, even from retirement; and Colleen for putting up with me during this longer than expected process.

"Times are bad, children no longer obey their parents, and everyone is writing a book."

— Marcus Tullius Cicero (106-43 BC)
Statesman, orator, and writer

Contents

"Never carry your shotgun
or your knowledge at half cock."

— *Austin O'Malley (1858-1932)*
American oculist

Preface

I am writing the preface for this book with my laptop siting on an elegant, yet very weathered, thirty-foot long cherrywood bar once patroned by Butch Cassidy; where no one carried their shotgun at half cock.

In those days many men sought wealth from the silver, zinc, copper, and gold mines of the area, although Butch Cassidy was likely not thinking of mining as he sipped whiskey at this bar. Those men, like all of us today, sought to achieve a competitive advantage in whatever occupation they toiled in.

In the early days here in the San Juan mountains of Telluride, Colorado, men sought current and reliable data regarding what mines were in production and how many ounces of metal were recently mined. They sought knowledge from their peers and suppliers on the latest mining techniques, such as which blasting fuse worked best in what situation.

They sought that knowledge, as we do today, in order to achieve a competitive advantage in their market. Achieving that advantage is what this book is all about.

I have read many books on information management and today's new twist, *knowledge management*, mostly with disappointment.

Many of these books are written by scholars who focus far too much valuable time on theory and the written version of the sound-byte. They come up with new terms for the same issues and processes. All that is fine if your goal is a thesis, but it is mostly a waste of time for those of us who struggle with real world issues in today's increasingly competitive business environment.

With that in mind, I have focused on providing real guidance that you can use immediately. Your project, program, prototype, initiative, or strategic thrust will succeed or fail based on technical, managerial, and cultural issues, not on information theory.

That is not to say that all definitions and descriptions are irrelevant. Effectively managing *knowledge, information,* and *data* is discussed in detail throughout this book. There is a real distinction between what these three words represent, and it is important to understand that distinction as you attempt to efficiently manage each of them.

Structured and *unstructured* information is also discussed, not because one can fill a chapter on describing the differences, but because the way we effectively manage that content is fundamentally different. Likewise, the distinction between a *document* and a *record* has important implementation differences, not to mention legal consequences, which many people unfortunately overlook.

Most of the effort required to achieve nirvana (the ultimate of attained wisdom) does not involve technology. Instead, it involves the challenges of effectively managing, and often altering, an organization's culture, complete with all the social, political, and knowledge-hoarding issues, as well as turf wars and a true need to think outside of the box.

Achieving Knowledge Nirvana in an enterprise is the most difficult initiative one can undertake. This book will greatly assist in that quest, but will not solve the issues or provide all the guidance one will need. Having undertaken many such initiatives for my clients over the past two decades, from a decision support solution encompassing workgroups on three continents, to a simple workflow application for the tomato industry of western Spain, I have had to overcome these and many other challenges.

This book is focused on achieving organizational success. This may be measured by obtaining a competitive advantage in your market, or even accelerating your organization's cycle of innovation, so imperative in today's information-based economy. Both of these are attainable through various means. However, the most direct approach is to optimize what we already have: our employees and our intellectual assets. Truly optimizing them, along with their related processes and enterprise content, will have a transformational effect on the organization, increasing innovation and differentiating the organization from competitors.

In this book, I trust that I have adequately conveyed the real challenges that one will face, along with the guidance and lessons learned that are necessary to overcome them. I have certainly toiled with this for a long time, mostly with success, although even the failures have resulted in a better understanding of those critical issues that, if not overcome, will kill a project.

Additional information will be posted on the Knowledge Nirvana web site, located at KnowldgeNirvana.com.

Jüris Kelley
October 14, 2001
Telluride, Colorado

"There is much pleasure to be gained
from useless knowledge."

—*Bertrand Russell (1872-1970)*

Chapter One

Introduction

U seless knowledge. That's the outcome of most knowledge management initiatives, decision support systems, and related collaboration solutions after six months from implementation. Whether you have built a groupware application for the collaboration of the various communities of practice within your enterprise, or a portal for single-source access to your organization's intellectual capital, failure is not only common, but likely.

Why is this? Why do most of these initiatives fail?

They fail because the objective is elusive and, simply put, it is difficult to implement successfully and sustain over time. You have technical integration issues to overcome, such as data extraction tools for legacy databases and even interoperability problems with the various operating systems that are encountered throughout a large enterprise. There exists a multitude of content sources that need to be effectively managed, including both structured data and unstructured information repositories.

Then there are my two favorite reasons that lead one down the path of inevitable failure: knowledge decay and discovery risk. We rarely address the legal issues and ramifications associated with content management and employee collaboration. This oversight is closely followed by those who focus their efforts on structured "knowledge" residing in databases, yet all but ignore the document, which is the default container of most information.

By far the greatest challenge, however, is cultural resistance. There exists today, and will remain tomorrow, a fundamental conflict between the hoarding and sharing of information. Cultural issues do not end there, however. We must also effectively manage the processes that form the foundation of any enterprise. Even if you do not attempt to optimize the process through a process improvement initiative, you will still be faced with the often significant variance between what management believes is the current business process and what reality often is.

知

What really is knowledge management (KM)? It certainly is a hot topic in both business and the IT industry, and we have all been told that we should be implementing it. Yet KM has few reliable descriptions and even fewer tangible solutions. It is not just a portal software product or a content management application, nor is it simply a workflow tool.

Can one even manage knowledge, or are we just providing information management solutions under a new term—an inflation of terms? What about content management? Is it yet another name for the same technology?

This book will answer those questions and will put the terms and concepts into perspective.

More importantly, however, this book provides you with the guidance necessary to implement a successful set of solutions that is critical for an enterprise to leverage its knowledge to achieve a competitive advantage in today's economy.

This book is light on the hypothetical and heavy on guidance and lessons learned during real implementations, some successful and others not. It focuses on the hard issues—those that if not overcome will kill your project. As one who has lived his professional life implementing such solutions for a wide variety of industries, I have a great appreciation for the multitude of issues that can kill such a project.

You may be reading this book because you are exploring the

possibility of implementing a portal product, a content management system, or other such collaboration solutions for your enterprise. Or you may already be involved in a less-than-stellar project that is having its difficulties and are seeking ideas for its salvation. Either way, this book will be important in your understanding of the mostly non-technical issues, such as cultural acceptance; ensuring knowledge sharing; and managing for knowledge decay, which are all crucial to success.

Not understanding and managing these issues, as well as the other risks that are identified and discussed in this book, will ensure failure.

Let's review a quick outline of the book's contents. Get your highlighter pen ready, sit up straight, think, and let's get going.

知

I have tried to keep the paragraphs fairly short, allowing you the opportunity to digest each major topic in relatively short time-frames. This should be accommodating to most of you—the hurried business or technical practitioner. I have also tried not to be too winded, going for more precise information content and useful guidance as opposed to having voluminous chapters that read like a Tom Clancy novel.

Furthermore, this book is not so much a technical reference as it is a management book. I have purposely not dived into the details of specific products; that is what trade magazine reviews and industry technical reports provide. With most software product vendors planning a new release every three to six months, it is impossible to articulate accurate information regarding product reviews or related advice in any book. Besides, the real issues that we must address—the hard issues—are not technical at all.

Here is how the book is organized.

Following this introductory chapter, we start off with the first major section of the book, which focuses on *content & risk*. This begins with a discussion of the issues, challenges, and relevant solutions that are available to you. Chapter two, *At the Speed of*

Thought, focuses on the business objectives and challenges to achieving the competitive advantage. The four pillars of optimization—or Knowledge Nirvana—are discussed. These are content, people, processes, and technology.

Chapter three, *Data, Information, and Knowledge*, distinguishes between these terms and answers the question, "can we manage knowledge?" Chapter four, *Structured and Unstructured Data*, along with chapter five, *Documents Versus Records*, are very important to one's understanding of what we are managing and how to manage it.

Discovery Risk and Knowledge Decay in chapter six describes what happens to knowledge, information, and data over time in terms of its usefulness for business decision making. Discovery risk discusses the very real and dangerous consequences of keeping any content in easily accessible forms—easily accessible, that is, for an auditor or the opposing counsel in a lawsuit.

Chapter seven, *Communities of Practice*, discusses how people naturally form groups that collect, share, and otherwise hoard information. Chapter eight, *Prospecting for Knowledge*, describes how you and others in your organization should seek out knowledge throughout the enterprise. How users can "self service" the content is described along with information harvesting techniques.

The next four chapters comprise the second major section of the book, which focuses on *collaboration, culture,* and *processes.* This includes chapter nine, *Collaboration—It's a Funny Thing*, followed by *The Great Impediment: Cultural Acceptance,* which discusses the most important hurdle one faces in any such implementation. Chapter eleven, *Work Process Automation,* offers the means to manage processes throughout the enterprise. Chapter twelve, *Process Improvement*, covers the key issues of how much process improvement or business process reengineering (BPR) you should conduct, and just how this should be accomplished.

The next five chapters represent more of a solutions perspective and encompass the third and final section of this book, entitled *Implementing Successful Solutions.*

This section starts with chapter thirteen, *Enterprise Portal Solutions*, describing what often represents the real KM solution—a portal application. This is followed by a chapter on how to import information, manage the repository, and dispose of outdated information. This chapter is entitled *Feeding the Portal*. Chapter fifteen, *Web Content Management*, discusses a similar yet somewhat different challenge—managing Internet-based content in a large enterprise.

Chapter sixteen, *Successful Project Planning*, discusses some of the basics that we often overlook in project management, as well as providing content and collaboration-specific project implementation advice. It also outlines what you should look for in software products and their vendors, how integrators can add real value to your initiative, and how to use consultants successfully while remaining financially liquid.

Chapter seventeen, *The Knowledge Nirvana Methodology*, covers an enterprise-wide methodology that is useful for implementing such systems.

Finally, chapter eighteen, *95 Knowledge Nuggets (Tips) for Success*, provides a compendium of 95 tips, more fashionably known as "knowledge nuggets."

知

Following this final chapter is a prologue written after the shocking events of September 11, 2001. The attacks on the World Trade Center and the Pentagon that day shattered our sense of security. It was an attack on our civil infrastructure, by a weapon of mass destruction, disruption, and destabilization.

Those who guard our homeland from such attacks suffer from the same knowledge, content, and collaboration issues that commercial enterprises do. It is remarkable how similar the issues, challenges, and even solutions are.

Fighting terrorism is a team endeavor, and as with any team that strives for success, one must achieve knowledge sharing, efficient collaboration, and effective content management. The guardians of our homeland lacked the will to do the right thing—to share knowledge, promote collaboration, and manage content—and that led to one set of terrorists that got through.

There are those who have called the events of September 11th an *information failure*, and they may be right.

Fortunately, content and collaboration technologies, along with KM in general, is now recognized by many as the enabling technology required for successful Homeland Security and our War on Terrorism.

When you finish this book, you will have gained a real understanding of the critical issues that one encounters in the real world of content and collaboration management.

A lot of work will be required to implement your solution successfully. You will spend countless hours helping employees through a pilot implementation. You will face scrutiny in justifying the business case and the return on investment. You will encounter those who hoard information and those who will be just shy of being openly hostile to any idea of sharing their knowledge with others. Software product vendors will mislead you about product claims and some in your organization may seek any angle necessary to increase their power, even if it means sacrificing your project.

You may encounter, as I have, union issues that seem insurmountable. You may uncover illegal activity as you develop your "as-is" process models. These are the challenges we face in our quest to implement successful IT solutions to manage enterprise content and optimize employee collaboration.

Section One

Content
& Risk

"Managing knowledge is not something you do. It's a perspective on problem solving that enables the organization to use what it collectively knows to tackle the complex, strategic problems."

— David S. Clarke
Director of IT Operations & Infrastructure
General Motors North America

Chapter Two

At the Speed of Thought

We live in an era of efficiency. No longer are we wildly optimistic about the Internet, spending extravagantly in the name of market share. Today's organizations are looking inwardly, focusing on the efficiency of their enterprise.

Improving internal efficiency is the least expensive way to obtain the competitive advantage. It does not require significant technical breakthroughs or risky partnerships with those in your extended supply chain. Instead, it is attainable by managing the content resources, which the organization has already assembled, and by optimizing the collaboration of its employees. Employees work in the many communities of practice (CoP) that exist, overtly and covertly, throughout your organization. They work with, create, and modify content and utilize processes that are at the heart of the enterprise.

Achieving the competitive advantage is necessary for survival in today's fluid business environment. The volume, velocity, and variety of information crossing your desk is overwhelming. Markets are rapidly changing, and so is the competition in our rapidly evolving economy. Today, we act at the speed of thought.

知

It is often said that people are an organization's most valuable asset. While that remains true for some, the pendulum has swung towards the organization's other key asset: information, or, more accurately stated, "content."

There may be those who disagree. There are those who are quick to point to the Internet's vast holding of content and how useless it can seem as one drowns in data yet thirsts for information. Those people, however, do a great injustice to the modern knowledge management tools and related solutions that can be used to harvest valuable information from vast content repositories. They are like the Luddites of the British industrial revolution who opposed technological change; they will even destroy any laborsaving system that may diminish their sense of employment.

Knowledge management (KM) is not so much about managing tacit (existing) institutional knowledge as it is about managing the disparate content sources and providing information-harvesting capabilities to our teams. KM is about optimizing the communities of practice or other workgroups and enabling them, through Information Technology (IT), to efficiently manage the enterprise's content and their own workgroup practices and procedures. KM attempts to eliminate the continuous reinvention of the wheel by providing repositories of best practices and knowledge nuggets. A KM toolkit provides us with the ability to efficiently gather, contribute to, organize, distribute, collaborate, and refine information.

We focus on information for a reason, for knowledge itself happens only when human experience and insight is applied to data and information. As Charles West Churchman concluded over thirty years ago, "Knowledge resides in the user and not in the collection of information. It is how the user reacts to a collection of information that matters."

Our goals, therefore, are to leverage the knowledge held by our employees (often referred to as "corporate memory") and make effective use of enterprise content to enable others to efficiently create knowledge themselves.

知

Even though I am more of a practitioner than a theoretician, I am often asked for a definition of KM. I must first admit that I am not a big fan of that term, for it is impossible to manage *knowledge*. KM is more of a "new economy" buzzword than anything else. If you want to call the concepts of effectively managing content and collaboration *knowledge management*, then so be it.

With that in mind, I have assembled a definition. One sentence would not quite do, so provided below is an expanded definition.

Knowledge Management is a concept that combines content (data and information) with organizational processes and people, as well as the technologies that enable their effective use. It is a concept only, for we cannot manage knowledge itself. Knowledge exists between our ears. What is both attainable and desirable in today's information-based economy is to provide the right content to the right people at the right time, thus allowing one to leverage their tacit knowledge with timely content to effect organizational decision making for a competitive advantage. KM is the fusion of content, people, processes, and technology.

From an IT perspective, KM combines records management, databases, workflow, and middleware tools, along with collaborative concepts and process improvement philosophies.

It is important to recognize that KM is a concept, or as others have suggested, a management practice, or notion, or process. It clearly is not a software product, or a technology, or any single methodology.

Knowledge is something that has been widely discussed in religion as well as in scholarly and political pursuits throughout history. "All genuine knowledge originates in direct experience," wrote Chairman Mao Tse-tung in his *On Practice* in 1937. Similarly, Islam discusses knowledge in some detail. The Qur'an teaches that knowledge depends on the use of our sight, hearing, intelligence, and other senses. It further correlates the stages of human existence with the three sources of knowledge.

Whether the Qur'an, the Bible, or the teachings of Chairman Mao, they would all agree that knowledge is not manageable, and it certainly does not reside in an e-mail or a database.

知

Content represents one of the four pillars that must be effectively managed and optimized throughout the enterprise. The other three pillars are people, processes, and technology. These four represent the four pillars of Knowledge Nirvana.

The need to optimize our data and information content should be intuitive. However most organizations today only effectively manage their operational data, so long as it resides in a database. The document is the default format in which we create, store, and share information, and most of these documents reside on unmanaged PCs.

Improving employee efficiency is yet another area in which most organizations need drastic help. Employees can walk out the door at any time to work for a competitor in our *at-will* employment environment, taking with them your organization's corporate memory. This issue is only subjectively addressed by most organizations.

Processes, either structured or ad-hoc, are at the heart of any functioning enterprise. Content is the subject of most processes and may reside within the process.

Processes, especially the ad-hoc informal processes, build a trust relationship between those in the organization that may not be apparent to management or even to themselves. This *social network* builds trust between people much quicker than formal, mandated, processes ever could.

Finally, technology, which is the great enabler that allows us to achieve our goals, compresses the time and effort of processes and allows us to effectively manage enterprise content.

There are many such technologies at our disposal. Document

and records management repositories are useful for the majority of unstructured content. Workflow products allow us to manage processes. Portals, although a generic term that is comprised of many technologies, represent a key software solution that all enterprises should leverage today.

Decision support systems, which have been used for well over a decade, attempt to aggregate large quantities of structured data to drive automated analysis and provide decision options to management.

Like portals, decision support systems, which are also referred to as *business intelligence systems*, are really a generic term for a number of technologies, techniques, and specific software tools that attempt to support cognitive reasoning. Decision support systems are usually comprised of tools and applications that perform data extraction, transformation, data load tools, data warehousing, data modeling, and query and reporting capability.

When faced with an issue, people can efficiently think cognitively and intuitively, using their decision-making skills to assess the situation and establish a course of action. People easily use cognitive reasoning (learning from the past to make decisions for the future).

Decision support systems, however, have failed to support cognitive decision-making. This is largely due to their limitations to act in real time. Today's online environment, in which we act at the speed of thought, has all but shattered the dream of automating the decision process. Nevertheless, the technologies developed and refined over the years under the banner of *decision support systems* are invaluable today as tools that perform functions such as data extraction and transformation.

知

Knowledge is power; therefore managing knowledge efficiently represents nirvana in today's rapid business and cultural environment. Achieving Knowledge Nirvana, however, requires careful planning and the use of a sound strategy and defined methodology.

Not to utilize a proven strategy or methodology is to reinvent the wheel. The Knowledge Nirvana methodology, which is an enterprise-wide methodology, along with key principals and best practices, is covered in chapter seventeen.

"The word knowledge, strictly employed, implies three things, viz., truth, proof, and conviction."

— *Richard Whately (1787-1863)*
Archbishop of Dublin

Chapter Three

Data, Information, and Knowledge

If you studied information technology in college, such as computer science or information systems, you learned the difference between *data* and *information*. This is literally Computer Science 101. Now, however, we have appended onto this fundamental distinction the term *knowledge*.

What exactly is knowledge? Can one differentiate between knowledge and information? Or is the term knowledge, especially *knowledge management,* just a fad created by software companies which are always looking for a reason to sell you the newest version of their product? It is important to understand these distinctions as you define your content sources and their characteristics.

知

Let's start with simple definitions of *data, information*, and *knowledge.*

Data is comprised of the basic, unrefined, and generally unfiltered information. An example of data is a customer contact list. This list has data elements, such as first names; last names; and zip codes. When reviewing the quality of this data, one is only interested in assuring that the data is complete and accurate; e.g., no missing zip codes or misspelling of a customer's last name.

Webster's Ninth New Collegiate Dictionary defines data as "factual information (as measurements or statistics) used as a basis for reasoning, discussion, or calculation."

Information, on the other hand, is much more refined data. It is data that has evolved to the point of being useful for some form of analysis. When you analyze various data elements together and produce some form of conclusion, you have turned data into information.

Using our simple customer list, if you reviewed raw sales data, such as what products were sold during the last year, and correlated that with the zip codes of the customer list, you would be able to produce a report that showed sales information by demographic regions. This would be useful information to a sales manager.

A rookie salesman would take that report and attempt to analyze it, looking for patterns as he tries to understand why sales in his region did not meet expectations. The seasoned sales manager, on the other hand, is able to look at that same report and immediately understand why sales were down. That sales manager is using her knowledge to interpret and understand the information in the report. That is the difference between *information* and *knowledge.* Without our human understanding that comes from personal context, all we have is data.

Truth, proof, and conviction—the three requirements articulated by Archbishop Whately (see quote at beginning of chapter)—is what the sales manager has that the rookie salesman does not. The sales manager has seen many similar reports over the years and has firsthand experience in the field working with customers. She knows regional sales cycles and other critical factors that influence sales. She believes her instinct, the truth of why the sales are what they are; she has the proof, in previous sales reports over the years; and she has the conviction that she is correct.

So how do you manage that knowledge—that knowledge that exists between the ears of that sales manager? You don't. You must, however, do the next best thing: manage the organization's information in such a way as to make it readily accessible and easily interpretable by others. This, along with optimizing the organization's processes, will facilitate knowledge creation and sharing, and will lead to an acceleration of the cycle of innovation.

知

Let's now look at what makes up the basis of the sales manager's knowledge as she reviewed that most recent sales report.

First, she had historical information from years of previous sales reports. While she certainly did not remember all the numbers, she did remember the basis of the reports; e.g., what areas increased sales at what times of the year.

She also had access to a wealth of other information, such as what brands sold well during certain months and what competitors were doing. She also realized that many people are on vacation in August and are not, therefore, around to purchase their products. All of this data and information is easily analyzed by the experienced sales manager.

The data and information that she used is most likely available to others in her organization. They simply have not had the time to read it all, let alone analyze it to the extent necessary to establish the truth, proof, and conviction that the seasoned sales manager has.

All of this data and information exists in:

- Structured databases—containing raw data, such as customer lists and sales figures.
- Database reports—generated from the raw data and usually show totals and summary data.
- Sales reports—show what has been sold to whom. Also contains information such as what the employees are finding in the field about customer preferences and the competition.
- E-mail—to and from different sales personnel and to sales and production management regarding quality issues raised during customer calls.
- Marketing plans—formal documents that outline the plans of the organization.

- Memoranda—documents outlining various successes, issues, and operational problems.
- Reports—documents that present analysis of topics, such as production runs or competitive analysis.

This partial list takes many forms and resides in many content repositories, to include: structured databases; document and records management systems; e-mail applications; and file systems. It includes both structured and unstructured content, which is discussed in chapter four.

By this time you should have a fairly good appreciation for what your challenge is. You must manage many different types of data and information which reside in many different forms and repositories. Worse yet, your competition is the human brain—the brain of that sales manager who has already performed the analysis and established her conviction.

So what do you do? Giving up is not an option. The workforce today is too fluid; the competition too real. Effectively harnessing information is imperative for survival.

Efficiently managing a collection of data and information to achieve a competitive advantage comes down to managing content smartly and optimizing the collaboration between employees in the organization. Put more simply, you must manage people, processes, the enabling technology that employees use, and the information that they generate.

There are many ways to accomplish this. Document and records management systems are good at managing the unstructured data that exists in documents such as Microsoft Word, PowerPoint, and Excel. These systems can also manage hardcopy (paper) documents that are either stored in file cabinets or are scanned as images, usually as Tagged Image File Format (TIFF) files.

Structured data is efficiently managed in databases. These databases can easily produce reports based on the data, but they provide very little useful information without being correlated with other information sources. One can also utilize data mining tools that assist in uncovering otherwise difficult to ascertain patterns within the data.

E-mail poses a challenge, since it is comprised of both structured and unstructured date. The structured data elements are typically the *to*, *from*, and *subject* fields, along with the data and time stamp for each e-mail. The unstructured data, where the useful information likely resides, is in an unstructured text portion of the e-mail body, which may also contain other elements, such as graphics; hyperlinks; and embedded files.

While e-mail provides a form of collaboration, so do discussion threads that are found in *groupware* applications. These are semi-structured discussions involving members of specific communities of practice. One can add their thoughts to the discussion or pose a question to the members of that discussion group.

Complementing data and information are *processes*. A process is a series of actions or functions performed to complete an operation. Processes are the lifeblood of an organization. They may be formally defined and well documented or informal in nature and only understood by the few employees who perform the process.

The processes of an organization eventually determine the method and type of collection of much of the data and information upon which we rely. These processes may include *best practices* of an organization that represent optimized processes to be used throughout the enterprise.

Attempting to combine the various repositories (databases, document management systems, e-mail, and groupware) are *portals*. A portal provides a single interface into multiple repositories. The user can run a single query and receive a single list of results. The results are brief descriptions of the content, with pointers back into the various repositories that contain the actual content.

知

It should be clear that there is no one solution to managing data, information, and knowledge, as well as the related processes that must also be effectively managed. Instead, there are a number of technologies and tools you may use, as has been described in this chapter and later throughout this book.

In this quest there are those who have tried other methods, such as videotaping knowledgeable employees discussing their jobs, explaining how they make decisions. Videotaping employees who are about to leave the organization, usually through retirement, is yet another method for capturing this critical information. It has limited use, however, since there is no efficient way to search and retrieve this information on any granular level.

Portals, however, are discussed in detail in chapter thirteen. Portals are the single best solution we have for managing enterprise information. They represent one of the few software products available today from which every organization can benefit.

"Some people drink
from the fountain of knowledge,
others just gargle."

— *Robert Newton Anthony*
American writer and author

Chapter Four

Structured and Unstructured Data

Whether you are dealing with data or information, all of this content falls into one of two categories: *structured* or *unstructured*. Understanding the difference between the two is crucial to implementing an effective system to manage the content and harness the information within.

Structured data is by far the easiest with which to work. Going back to the previous chapter's customer database example, structured data would include the customer's first name, last name, and zip code. This data is neatly organized in a database, made up of records and fields. Because the fields are pre-defined, such as a 15-character alphanumeric field for the last name (a field that contains both characters and numbers), or a 9-character numeric field for the zip code, the database application can efficiently store, sort, retrieve, and report on this data. It knows what to expect of the data, and it knows how to efficiently manage it.

While every modern enterprise today relies on databases for storing its massive amount of mission-critical data, most information does not reside in databases. Many studies over the years have shown that upwards of 93 percent of all corporate information resides in unstructured forms. It is these unstructured content containers that are much more difficult to manage.

To use another analogy, every organization has a Chief Financial Officer (CFO) who uses some form of accounting and financial system. This system is a database that contains structured financial data. Reports are run on this raw data. These reports are analyzed by the CFO, who produces memoranda and briefings on topics such as what expenses are too high and what accounts are in trouble. These memoranda and reports contain valuable information to the organization. These memos are likely unstructured Word documents, and the reports are likely unstructured PowerPoint documents.

Therefore the CFO relies on the financial system for the basic data and reports generated by that system, but uses his own personal knowledge to craft an information-based memo. That memo is unstructured content and must also be managed whether it is a Word document or an e-mail.

知

Most information today contains unstructured content. Think about where you create and store most of your information. Do you spend hours entering information into structured databases every day? Of course not. If you are like most people, you spend your day composing word-processing documents, spreadsheets, and probably PowerPoint presentations. And who could forget e-mail? The informational content of e-mail is mostly unstructured text.

Now comes the scary part. Where does most of this unstructured content reside? Answer: on the local hard disk drive of your desktop or laptop PC. Sure, e-mail sits on a server, hopefully managed and backed-up by your IT staff, but most information, certainly the important information, probably resides on your local drive in a Word document.

Think about it. All of this valuable information resides in an inaccessible drive in a format that is, at best, difficult to search.

If you do nothing else, the most cost-effective action you can take is to simply abolish content (data files) from local disk drives and put them into a robust centralized document management system. This will allow every employee who has the appropriate security permission (and the need-to-know) to access this valuable information with easy-to-use search and retrieval tools.

Unstructured content, however, consists of much more than Word documents. It also includes graphical files (e.g., .jpg and .bmp file formats), video, and voice clips.

Besides having video as independent files, they, along with graphics, are embedded into other files. These *compound documents* are discussed in chapter five, *Documents Versus Records*. What is important at this point is to be able to search, retrieve, and reuse content throughout the enterprise.

知

Let's explore searching and retrieving unstructured content. Reusing the data, once you have it, is not that difficult today. Cut and paste functionality is powerful within the Microsoft Office suite of applications, so reusing data is not a concern like it once was.

If you think about any file of unstructured data—a Word document, an HTML file, a PDF file, or a TIFF document image—they all have some form of metadata that may be useful. Metadata is data about data, and provides the information map for a repository.

There are really two types of metadata, both equally important. The first is the business view of metadata, which describes the fields, such as first name; last name; and zip code. The second type of metadata is the technical view. This describes important aspects of the data, such as when the data was created; by whom; when was it last updated; and who owns the data.

A Word document allows the user to enter basic metadata, such as the author; date; subject; and a brief description. You can and should use these fields that are embedded within the Word document. Many search tools, which will be discussed later, can be configured to use Word's metadata fields to search upon.

An HTML file, which is the foundation of most Internet documents, is really just a flat file. Like Word files, HTML embeds metadata fields internally. TIFF files, which are the most common file format for document images, also embed some limited data within the file, called the *TIFF Header*.

As you can see from these examples, almost all unstructured data resides in file formats that use some sort of metadata to help the user manage and search on the content embedded within the file.

知

Searching on unstructured content can generally be performed in one of two ways. One method is to search the metadata either associated with the individual file or contained within the file.

Like structured data in a database, this metadata is of a fixed type and size and is, therefore, more efficient to search on. Search engines designed for this type of search could simply be Microsoft Word itself pointed towards a file directory. This works relatively well for those who have one file type, such as Word.

There are also other search engines that understand the proprietary file formats of Word and other formats, as well as industry standard formats such as TIFF. The capability to search this wide variety of file types is usually found in document management systems, also known as *integrated document management* (IDM); *enterprise document management systems* (EDMS); *records management* applications; or just advanced versions of *imaging systems.*

Any of these refined searches—that search on metadata fields—are generally superior to using the alternative, which is the *full-text search.*

知

The popular phrase "drowning in data, starving for information" accurately describes the frustrating results of most full-text searches. In fact, most information today is just clutter.

Full-text searches generally perform a simple text search comparison on the ASCII text found within a file.

A simple example of a full-text search is a search on the Internet. When using Internet-based portals, such as Yahoo or Google, you are usually performing a full-text search on the text index that Yahoo has created based on the ASCII text of HTML files.

We have all entered a simple query only to be confronted with thousands of "hits." Not only is this an overwhelming amount of data, but the search engine is not capable of distinguishing between *Star Wars* and *Ronald Reagan* and *Star Wars* and *George Lucas*.

When assessing the accuracy of hits, there are two factors to consider, precision and recall. Precision is the accuracy of the documents identified that are relevant to your search. For example, the hit list returned 100 documents, but only 20 were relevant. Recall, on the other hand, is a measure of the number of documents that were accurately identified from the repository. The hit list returned 30 documents when there were actually 50 relevant documents.

Precision and recall are the two factors used to measure the accuracy of a search result. While it is fairly easy to gage the precision—you know how many documents were not what you wanted—recall is difficult to measure because you typically do not know the relevancy of the entire collection in the repository.

As mentioned earlier, most Internet search engines scan HTML files and create an inverted index of the words within the source document. This is known as *spidering* a repository. Some words, such as "a" and "the" are known as *stop words* and are omitted due to their frequent use and low value in a search.

Note that full-text search engines are by no means limited to the Internet. Even before the mass acceptance of the Internet, full-text search engine products were widely used by organizations that needed to search large unstructured document collections. These products allow you to perform a relatively fast search on large document collections containing many formats.

There are, however, many other forms of search techniques that are more advanced than the reverse index. Most of these are based on some form of *pattern matching*.

Pattern matching techniques, such as those based on non-linear adaptive digital signal processing, identify the patterns that occur in text. The letters, words, and sentences are analyzed based on their use and frequency and are correlated to words that correspond to specific ideas or concepts. This allows a pattern matching search engine to extract the concept of a document's content. Not only can one perform more accurate searches, but this technology can also be used to conduct near real-time analysis of documents that are in a repository. This is useful for mass categorization of an enterprise's content.

知

Do not assume that all of your mission-critical information is safely managed in a corporate database. The truth is quite the contrary. Your valuable information sits on local disk drives that probably are not even backed-up. Don't forget that these drives include laptops that are easily stolen or misplaced.

It is important to understand what forms of content you have to contend with. This will dictate what kind of tools you will need to harvest the knowledge contained within your organization. You also need to consider what level of granularity you need to effectively search on. Do you need—or more likely, can you afford—to only use a full-text search? These are several of the many questions that you will need to ask yourself as you analyze the multitude of data, file, and format types that contain your organization's critical content.

"Identify your records as early as possible, deleting those that should be deleted; do so before it becomes too late."

—William S. Bivens
Document Imaging and Records Pioneer

Chapter Five

Documents Versus Records

The previous chapter discussed the important distinction between structured and unstructured content. Similarly, this chapter explains yet another important distinction—one that has legal implications: the difference between a *document* and a *record*.

Let's first discuss what a document is. A document is any container of data or information. It is described as a container because it is usually a unique file with a certain format that contains content.

There could be any number of data types within the container, such as text; graphics; linked charts; video; or audio. From the document perspective, it really does not matter what is contained within the document.

Remember that a document includes e-mail. Each e-mail message is really a document; i.e., it is an individual file with a certain format that contains content. Similarly, database reports, when the report is run, also produce individual files that can be stored or printed.

A document, therefore, can be anything from a simple spreadsheet to an e-mail that contains embedded files, including a voice clip from the e-mail's sender.

These mixed-media documents (also called Compound Documents) pose some interesting challenges, such as how you print that e-mail with the voice clip. What is printed is not the document in its entirety, for the document contains a voice clip. What about a document with a digital signature (used for authentication; not an actual signature)? How do you print that? As you can see, all this creates challenges.

知

One way to understand a document is to consider that each document has the following three key components: content; context; and structure.

Content is the subject matter of the documents, text, graphics, pictures, voice-clips, and video that resides within the document container. The content should be the same regardless of the medium; i.e., hardcopy paper or a softcopy document file.

Context referees the relationship of the document to something else, such as other documents or an action or event. The document context includes data about the creation, use, access, and storage of the document. Maintaining all three document components is important to ensuring the trustworthiness of a document. An e-mail that has been forwarded offers a good example of the need to understand the context of a document. If the original e-mail's header data fields (e.g., *to; from; subject;* and *date)* have been deleted, one may not understand the original context of the content now being forwarded. This puts the trustworthiness of this content into question.

The *structure* of a document defines what type of document it is; e.g., a letter or an e-mail. The structure will imply the typical types of attributes one would find on the document type, such as a date and a signature block embedded internally within the document. E-mail, on the other hand, has its attributes as metadata residing outside, or externally, of the document itself.

知

Now that you understand what a document is, let's discuss records. Every record is a document, but not all documents are records. A record is simply a document that has a special meaning associated with it.

A record is a document that is a recording of some action or decision that should serve as evidence of the transaction, decision, or action. The record has value because it is a recording of an ongoing operation, or it otherwise legally protects the organization's action or decision.

This could be a formal contract or, for example, an e-mail between management and the Human Resources department regarding the termination of an employee. Likewise, a record could be the Word document from Human Resources to the employee notifying him of his termination. Both of these are documents that have some important meaning pertaining to the organization's action or decision. That is a fairly vague definition, but defining which documents are records is vague when discussed in general.

All records, in order to be useful in documenting the action or decision, must be deemed trustworthy.

Some organizations have very specific definitions of what document constitutes a record. Government organizations, for example, have a multitude of laws and related rules that define what an "official record" is. Federal, state, and local governments all have personnel whose responsibility it is to determine what records are and how to preserve them. At the Federal level, these records are managed by The National Archives and Records Administration (NARA) in Washington, DC. NARA works closely with Records Managers in the various Federal agencies to ensure that the policies and procedures are implemented and that records are adequately maintained.

The government, however, isn't the only entity that strictly defines records. Any corporation that has legal matters—which is every one—has at least some form of defined records. Private organizations, such as the American Bar Association, are very active in defining records and related issues, such as preserving the trustworthiness of records and the use of digital signatures.

Along with legal requirements, any organization that is highly regulated by the government has a multitude of regulations defining what a record is and how to manage that record. This includes organizations such as utility companies, insurance companies, and the aerospace industry.

Organizations that take records management seriously develop a single set of policies and procedures to be applied consistently over the records collections. This is important legally, for those who later retrieve the records must be assured that the records are trustworthy.

Generally, a Records Manager has the responsibility of ensuring that the policies and procedures are faithfully implemented. Records are grouped into collections and are subject to the organization's records schedule. *Schedule* is a term that is used when determining which documents are records and how long those records are to be kept. For example, all contracts for office space may make up one schedule category and have a defined retention span of twenty years. Employee folders may be archived for seven years after the end of employment. After the seven years, the process would entail permanently deleting the folders.

Note that the employee folder may be a physical folder containing paper, or it may be an electronic folder consisting of Word documents and scanned TIFF images. In an automated records management system, the system itself would contain the logic to automatically delete the electronic employee folder immediately after the seven-year duration. This greatly improves the efficiency of the Record Manager and eliminates the need and expense of mass paper shredding.

Regardless of whether you have hardcopy or softcopy records, a records management system will assign a unique record identifier to every record. The system will uniformly create and manage an index that usually includes: a record identifier; a classification code; the creating individual; the creating organization; the subject; the media type; the date of the record; the address; the location of the record; and the record format.

As we become more reliant on purely softcopy documents—those documents that may live their entire life cycle online and

never be recorded on paper - we far surpass the existing legal definitions and processes that are well established in the paper world.
These issues are further discussed in chapter six, *Discovery Risk
and Knowledge Decay.*

On occasion, the courts get involved. A fairly recent event with
long-term implications took place at the end of the first George
Bush presidency. The staff of George H.W. Bush had planned to
delete all White House e-mails prior to President-elect Bill Clinton
taking office. Fortunately, the public interest group Public Citizen
filed a Federal lawsuit that eventually preserved the e-mails. From
that lengthy lawsuit, it became accepted practice to treat e-mail
documents as any other document, fully subject to all relevant
records requirements.

An example that we can all relate to involves voice mail. The
voice mail that most of us use is really audio files stored on a server
and managed by a voice mail application. So, as far as preserving
documents is concerned, what is the difference between a Word
document and a voice mail message? There is no difference. Both
need retention policies and procedures and are subject to scheduling to determine if they are in fact records.

知

Anytime you discuss records—those documents that must be
formally maintained—preservation inevitably becomes an issue.

As most first-time parents do, I bought a video camcorder to
record all those special moments of my son, Cullen. My video
collection is stored on about twenty VHS-C videotapes. I also
recorded some of his first words as a .wav file on my PC. Those
words can be replayed today, but will I be able to play that audio
back to Cullen twenty years from now? Probably not.

Disintegration and obsolescence will likely be the culprit of both
the VHS-C tapes and the .wav files, and it will also likely be the
culprit of most of your electronic documents.

Already, society is losing much of our modern recorded history.
NASA, for example, has permanently lost approximately twenty

percent of the data collected during the 1976 Viking voyage to Mars. NASA is not alone.

Disintegration of the media that records the files is one problem. Magnetic tapes may only last a decade. Floppy disks, videotapes, and hard drives are also vulnerable to magnetic fields, oxidation, humidity, dust, and material decay. Even CD-ROMs, which were once touted as lasting 100 years, appear to be much more vulnerable that previously assumed. Worse yet are the ultra inexpensive CD-ROMs. The adhesives that bind these disks can delaminate in only a few years, or even in a matter of months, making the data and information recorded on them useless.

Obsolescence is even a harder problem, for we have to overcome the obsolescence of the file format itself, plus the application that reads the file, the operating system that runs the application, and the hardware that both runs the operating system and reads the disk.

Stacked in the various corners of my office are unreadable zip disks that I purchased only three years ago. I also have WordStar word-processing files on 5.25" floppy disks that I don't have a prayer of ever retrieving. I also have a collection of proprietary, yet at the time very state of the art, 4mm tape cartridges that I used for backup only eight years ago.

知

What, then, is the solution to the disintegration and obsolescence of our documents? There really isn't any good solution. We are constantly embracing the newest, fastest, and most flexible technologies in the name of progress. Keeping up is economically impossible.

Now you can understand why professional archivists want you to stick with using paper.

There are, however, some general guidelines that you can follow as you address your organization's records preservation issues. These are:

- Store information in multiple formats.
- Avoid fads in media and formats, such as the latest Zip disk format that will likely be outdated in 18 months.
- Establish a migration plan for all your records and other critical content. Keep in mind the different types of migration needed; e.g., media, format, application, and operating system.
- Analyze the life cycle of each of your major record types.
- Backup everything to CD-ROM using only "CD-R" media, which offers the best hope of media non-obsolescence at this time.
- Like wine, keep all media in a cool, dry location, and avoid dust and magnetic fields.
- Don't discard that old hardware. Keep one or two copies of every type of hardware you have. This is a low cost insurance policy that you may need.

Establishment of a migration plan is probably the most important aspect of softcopy preservation.

A migration plan should take into account the life cycle of the content collection and all aspects necessary to retrieve and understand the context of each document. The currently used media, format, application, and operating system needs to be analyzed to determine when it should be migrated onto a newer version. The process for each conversion should be defined and performed in a formal manner.

In 1994 Congress determined that the Department of Defense did not have a comprehensive policy for electronic documents, records storage, or retention. I was asked to help create such a policy for the entire Department, including the tricky issue of preservation. The outcome of that project was a boldly entitled report called the "Master Plan" for documents and records. The plan was so complex and costly that everyone, including Congress, decided to ignore it. Not even Congress wanted to bring the issue up again.

知

There are many issues associated with documents and records, including legal; retention; and preservation. One could attempt to conquer them all, but that would not be economical.

One bright spot, however, is the ever-increasing functionality of enterprise-wide content management systems (covered later in this book). These systems allow you to manage content regardless of file type, and they take much of the burden off of manual entry of the required metadata. For an added bonus, you can use the records management features to perform your scheduling functions.

I often tell my clients that if you solve your other content requirements and implement a comprehensive system, then you can solve your records management issues at the same time. So you basically get records management for free. This not only gets the Records Management staff on-board in a hurry, but also alleviates the IT department's records concerns and adds to the return on investment of the overall project.

"You already have
zero privacy anyway.
Get over it."

— Scott McNealy
*Chairman, CEO, and co-founder
of Sun Microsystems*

Chapter Six

Discovery Risk and Knowledge Decay

Let's assume for a moment that you have overcome the cultural issues, upgraded the required infrastructure, and surmounted all other obstacles necessary to implement a comprehensive and widely used knowledge management system. Employee collaboration in the various communities of practice is going well, and you have successfully implemented an automated content management system that is efficiently controlling the organization's content. Life is sweet.

Having been promoted to an executive level position in your organization, you immediately recognize the deputy chief counsel as he knocks on the open door of your office. He has a request for you. The organization has been subpoenaed by a competitor. This competitor, who used to be a subcontractor for you, wants a copy of all records dealing with a software solution that was developed in-house for a current project. The competitor alleges that several senior technical employees in your organization misappropriated their software design trade secrets. The competitor has filed the subpoena in preparation for legal action.

The deputy chief counsel needs you to search your repository and provide him with a printout of all relevant records. "Surely there won't be much in that massive enterprise-wide repository, would there?" he asks, as your blood pressure quickly rises.

知

Scott McNealy's quote, "You already have zero privacy anyway. Get over it." is just as applicable to your content repository as it is to the business-to-consumer transactions to which McNealy was referring. Your repository, complete with discussion groups and saved draft documents, is a treasure trove for any opposing counsel. You have saved it all, the good and the bad, exposing your organization to the hoards of attorneys who would love to examine that content for their contract or tort civil action.

If you have the document or record, it is subject to discovery (the legal process by which attorneys "discover" what records exist during a dispute). There is no privacy. Get over it; or, more applicably, deal with it.

You have to deal with this issue, as well as a similar one—knowledge decay. Fortunately both can be overcome simultaneously as you solve your records management requirements.

知

Discovery risk and knowledge decay represent the two downsides of maintaining any organized repository of content. *Discovery risk* is the risk of keeping records that can be used against you in a legal action. *Knowledge decay* is the corroding in the relevancy of the content over time.

All content is perishable; its usefulness has a half-life. You have probably experienced the frustration of knowledge decay yourself. For example, in searching some corporate repository, either through a key-word search or by simply looking at file names in Microsoft Outlook's Public Folders, you find the files, only to discover that they are three years old and completely outdated. Those files have definitely been updated, but no one has bothered to update the repository. This is frustrating, and is the quickest way to turn a valuable asset into an application that no one in the organization bothers to use anymore.

You can probably see some parallels between the need to deal with knowledge decay and discovery risk and records management and content management.

The premise behind records management is to keep only what is needed and discard what is no longer needed or desired. You will solve much of the discovery issue when you apply records management functionality to your content repository. A key factor to remember is that you must not be arbitrary in what is kept and what is discarded. Otherwise, you will be subject to a very serious allegation of destruction of evidence, for one person's document is another person's evidence.

It cannot be emphasized enough that you must have a well-documented process with defined procedures for determining what is kept (scheduled) and what is discarded. This applies to documents and records in any format; i.e., softcopy, hardcopy, voice mail files, and e-mail.

Likewise, a content management system, which is described in chapter fifteen, helps ensure that the content is relevant and updated in a timely manner. Without an automated content management system, maintaining the content of any repository is a difficult and time-consuming task. This is the reason why so many repositories contain grossly out-of-date content and become useless; useless, that is, except to an opposing counsel.

知

A good example of the seriousness of and the direct costs associated with discovery of electronic content involved then-Vice President Albert Gore and the White House. The White House IT staff failed to keep thousands of e-mail records sent to hundreds of White House employees, including Vice President Gore. They did, however, have backup tapes. These tapes were at the file system level; hence, they were the raw files that comprised the e-mails and were not available in any structured or accessible manner via the e-mail application.

There were 4,025 tapes.

Congress subpoenaed the White House records during the course of an investigation. This subpoena encompassed all records, including e-mail.

Because the e-mails are records, they should have been scheduled and maintained in a formal records management system. They were not, however, as they were deleted in the e-mail application to free up disk space on servers. Because they were kept on backup tapes and thus subject to discovery, the White House had no choice but to restore all 4,025 tapes and then search them to produce the desired records for Congress.

This highly public failing is estimated to have taken six months and cost $3 million to reconstruct the e-mails and produce the subpoenaed records.

The lesson learned from the White House is that the stakes are high in both legal risk and the actual monetary costs associated with the compliance of subpoenas.

Your chief counsel will probably recommend one approach—deleting it all. IT professionals charged with establishing an employee collaboration system and providing knowledge repositories inevitably will take the opposite approach.

The solution is a fine line between the two, and is similar to what the records management profession has been preaching for years: you must schedule your documents and manage your records.

As you establish your content repository full of best practices, collaborative discussions, and knowledge nuggets, work with your chief counsel and those responsible for records management. Work with them from the beginning to implement records management functionality for your repositories early on, and let your chief counsel help define the business rules associated with the scheduling process. Doing so will alleviate two serious threats to your successful system deployment—discovery risk and knowledge decay.

"Every one wishes to have truth on his side, but it is not every one that sincerely wishes to be on the side of truth."

— Richard Whately (1787-1863)
Archbishop of Dublin

Chapter Seven

Communities of Practice

I n the course of our daily work, we typically interact with a variety of people, including our colleagues; managers; administrative assistants; and technical staff. We also interact with others outside of our department and organization, such as the accounting and shipping departments and external suppliers and vendors that comprise our supply chain. We communicate with whomever it takes to get the job done, to be successful, and to survive and prosper.

If these people are part a structured workgroup, such as when you order office supplies through your administrative assistant, your manager, the Accounting Department, and your office supply company, then you should have a work process predefined and use workflow tools to ensure process efficiency. Work process automation is discussed in chapter eleven.

There are other times, however, when your business interactions are not so structured.

If an urgent issue arises that must be addressed immediately, several people in your department may need to be involved in addressing the issue. You and your colleagues will probably contact others in your organization for answers and will search your Intranet repositories for clues as to who else may be able to assist. All these people are related in some manner to the issue being addressed; they have come together and formed an ad-hoc workgroup. If the issue occurs with some frequency, or is otherwise related to other issues or processes, then you are likely interacting with a *community of practice (CoP)*.

A CoP is a loose coalition of employees who share a similar interest or work process. They are usually self organizing and virtual in nature, cutting across vertical organizational boundaries. The CoP members are united by similar interests, values, and vocabulary and share a common purpose.

A cynic would say that a CoP is just another name for a *team*, but that doesn't fully describe the concept. A team is generally characterized as a defined group within an organization that is formed by management to work a certain objective. Key to this definition is that the team is mandated by others (usually management) and may include people who either provide no real value or don't want to be involved. Obviously this pessimism doesn't apply to all teams.

A CoP, on the other hand, is characterized by an informal relationship between colleagues who freely associate to share and learn. The CoP represents those people who have an active interest in a related topic. For this reason, the CoP may also be called a *community of interest*. The members come together voluntarily to share and learn from each other with candid dialogue. They operate on mutual trust and understanding.

Flourishing CoPs are a sign of a mature organization, and they provide one of the most effective mechanisms of knowledge sharing.

Northrop Grumman Corporation, for instance, has a CoP for knowledge management. It is comprised of several hundred people who come from all sorts of backgrounds, job descriptions, and locations. This "KM CoP" has employees who implement systems in Los Angeles, those who deploy systems for clients in Washington, and those who are users of internal systems. It includes technical personnel, management consultants, managers, and even those who simply have a passing interest in KM. The CoP interacts through a centralized content repository, a regularly published electronic newsletter, and an annual conference in Los Angeles. It is an active and diverse group that greatly enhances the corporate objectives and provides for efficient knowledge transfer.

It is important to have a face-to-face annual meeting. Despite the advances in e-mail and related collaboration tools, being able to interact socially and placing a real face with a name is important to strengthening the CoP and to promoting long-term sharing. Face-to-face bonding greatly helps everyone work together later in a virtual mode.

It is important to recognize the importance of CoPs. They exist, at least in some fashion, in every organization. For many, the CoPs, either formal or ad hoc, are how real work gets done.

Let's say that you have a storage compatibility technical issue that's preventing you from deploying a new Dell server. You're stumped and need assistance. You know who in your organization may be able to help, so you contact them for assistance. That informal list represents at least a partial CoP of employees in your organization who are knowledgeable about Dell servers. Everyone on that list has some mission, objective, task, or interest that is common to others; in this case, deploying Dell servers.

Think about how you work and with whom you interact. Are all the key employees that you depend on part of a defined and structured team? Probably not. Sure, there are teams, but other work, sometimes the majority of work, requires the interaction of informal groups. For some of you, especially those who would be characterized as "knowledge users," the majority of your work probably includes informal CoPs rather than defined teams.

As an IT professional, I am responsible for developing and deploying successful solutions for my clients. A project includes my project team, which is comprised of numerous programmers; systems analysts; business analysts; technical writers; and trainers. Each of them are assigned, by management, to the team.

I also have a wide variety of CoPs upon which I depend and to which I contribute in kind. For example:

- Senior Management CoP, which includes my management and their administrative assistants.
- Accounting CoP, which helps me with invoices and other financial issues that arise with a project.

- Contracting CoP, which includes contract specialists who handle the details of my client contracts, support attorneys, and financial analysts.

There are many more, but you get the point. I rely on these groups just as much as I do my assigned project team to resolve issues necessary to complete the project.

Now let's say that there are a number of managers like myself within the same organization who rely on the same list of support CoPs, such as Accounting and Contracting. Together, both the project managers and Accounting, for example, have similar interests and needs. Jointly we all could form a unified "Accounting CoP." These CoPs foster teamwork and efficiency, as well as help build a sense of community and trust.

知

CoPs are an important element of any organization, just as much as defined teams are. Therefore we need to support and enable the CoPs to ensure that they operate efficiently and effectively.

To do so, we first need to define which CoPs exist and then which are substantive and important enough to the organization's operations to warrant support. Performing this analysis is similar to work process automation analysis, but it needs to dig deeper into the organization's true workings.

You need to do more than define processes. You need to truly understand how an employee conducts their business. Who do they rely upon for information, either during the course of a typical process or during an exception, such as the difficulty with a Dell server?

To do so gets into the science of *social network analysis*. Social network analysis refers to the analysis of how a group, such as a work group, department, or organization, informally communicates. This social workflow can provide insight into how an organization truly conducts their business.

Performing a social analysis can provide an interesting insight into the organization's operations.

Let's say you have an organization that you are analyzing. You first perform work process analysis, described in chapter eleven, which will result in structured as-is process models. Performing a social analysis, however, may reveal a very different as-is model of information flow.

During one social analysis task I conducted, it was revealed that there existed a loose coalition of 14 people who relied upon one another for input and recommendations on key issues. This amounted to a covert work group that used back channels to communicate with one another.

In another example, a small office had defined workflows, but those workflows didn't represent the true information flow needed to process the work. In that case, it turned out that a manager, who appeared as a key decision-maker in the process, actually was generally bypassed for most information. Instead, several people depended upon an administrative support person for recommendations that were essential to the workflow. In this case, there did exist the official work process, but there also existed in parallel an informal process that was paramount to processing the workflow.

So what does social analysis have to do with CoPs and productivity in general? It is important to understand the true nature of data, information, and knowledge in the organization if we are to optimize that organization. A business process analysis task will define an apparently optimal work process, but only social network analysis will reveal the true information flow upon which the work process depends.

知

There are several ways to perform a social network analysis. The most straightforward way is to simply prod for true information flows and decision-making as you analyze the work processes. With this method, you perform your standard business process analysis, but also focus on true information flows and dependencies.

Another way, which is much more interesting, is to analyze e-mail traffic. This assumes, of course, that e-mail is the mechanism for most communications related to your area of interest.

Reviewing the frequency of sent and received e-mail on a given topic may reveal information flows that would not otherwise be obvious. It is important to recognize that one is not reading specific e-mail. When analyzing e-mail in this manner, simply review the frequency of sent and received e-mail on a given topic. You can determine the topic by simply searching for key words to look for patterns.

Analyzing e-mail was the only way in which the administrative support person was discovered as the workgroup member who was making the real recommendations. A graphical plot of all e-mail related to a specific process revealed a large number of e-mails going to that person, who was not formally part of the work process. Further, the e-mails were sent and received from those who were responsible for making recommendations, so it appeared as though they were e-mailing her prior to making a recommendation and subsequently continuing with the work process. Follow-up questioning by the analysis team confirmed the results of the analysis provided by the e-mail traffic.

Social network analysis in the business environment also goes well beyond simply defining otherwise hidden information flows. It can also reveal those who are impediments or roadblocks to information flow, as well as revealing the true knowledge sources or the real decision-makers.

知

As you can see from this chapter, CoPs exist in every organization. They are the often hidden resources that we depend on to solve our work responsibilities. Whether they are loosely coupled groups that rely on information exchange or covert channels of information flows, understanding CoPs is important as we optimize both content and collaboration throughout the enterprise. We must foster and support such efforts.

Supporting CoPs doesn't take much in terms of organizational support. It doesn't cost much, since they rely on self-organization and existing e-mail and workgroup repositories. A little support and the occasional face-to-face meeting is all that is needed; the payoffs can be substantial.

A man named Arthur Fry, who worked for 3M, was looking for a better way to mark the pages of his church choir's hymnals. He started collaborating with the adhesive CoP at 3M, which led to the development of the revolutionary Post-it Notes. Without the collaboration of Arthur Fry, Dr. Spence Silver, and Geoff Nicholson, the world would be without theses "sticky" notes that have become commonplace in offices and homes worldwide.

"It was the best of times,
it was the worst of times,
it was the age of wisdom,
it was the age of foolishness,
it was the epoch of belief,
it was the epoch of incredulity,
it was the season of light,
it was the season of darkness,
it was the spring of hope,
it was the winter of despair,
we had everything before us,
we had nothing before us,
we were all going directly to Heaven,
we were all going directly the other way."

– *Charles Dickens*

Chapter Eight

Prospecting for Knowledge

Prospecting for knowledge is like Charles Dickens' musings: "...we had everything before us, we had nothing before us...". We have vast knowledge before us, yet we are challenged to find it.

Employees accumulate knowledge—tacit knowledge—as they perform their jobs. They develop skills, certain expertise, and understandings during the course of their duties, both with their current employer and with prior employers. Most employees, consciously or not, have established their own "best practices." While this may be useful, it has limited value to the organization as a whole, for others must go through their own experiences and eventually build on their own lessons learned to create a set of best practices.

Making this tacit knowledge explicit is a key objective of any KM initiative; however, this is nearly impossible to achieve. While there are some occasions during which we attempt to capture and manage this tacit knowledge, which is described later in this chapter, we are left, for the most part, with a more humble objective of capturing the work products of those knowledge employees. In this respect, prospecting for knowledge is a little misleading, for one is not really seeking knowledge—one seeks content. Within that content resides critical business information that either forms the foundation for, or is used by, the knowledge that exists between our ears.

In this chapter, the challenges and pitfalls of acquiring content are addressed.

Most people focus on building an enterprise portal or other such application to manage their content. They have either performed a cost benefit analysis or have agreed to its intrinsic value, and so they proceed. Performing the requirements analysis, designing the architecture, building the application, and deploying the system is the relatively easy task. The real challenges are in acquiring the content and ensuring that the content remains relevant.

I worked with one large IT company on the east coast that decided to deploy a repository for one of their departments. It was clearly a good idea and could have offered great value to their employees and enhance departmental productivity. When the portal-based repository became operational, there was enthusiasm to populate it with content. That enthusiasm lasted about one week. After that, people had their "real jobs" to do and started neglecting the repository. This is a key challenge for most repositories: ensuring that content continuously gets contributed.

There are two primary ways to ensure that employees contribute content: the carrot and stick approach and the process approach. A third way, intimidation, has also been known to work.

The carrot and stick approach is intuitive and simple. Unfortunately, it also rarely works for very long. That east coast IT department, with their portal-based repository, used the carrot and stick approach. The portal was operational for about one month when they realized that it was getting harder and harder to get employees to contribute content. Some employees who had been enthusiastic when the repository first became operational began to significantly reduce the amount of content they were contributing.

Consequently, they had to be prodded with verbal requests for content. The time, and therefore the cost, of such prodding grew, and finally resulted in the need for a full-time system administrator. Management then tried another tactic. They started offering bounties, or rewards, for employee contributions. Posters were created and hung in the hallways and elevators announcing the rewards, which were in the form of a drawing for free travel. The grand prize was a free 3-day trip to Phoenix for two. Each contribution to the repository entitled that employee to one chance to win.

That was not a bad idea, as long as one recognizes that such an approach will have minimal and short-term impact. An organization cannot afford to offer such prizes forever, thus limiting the carrot. Furthermore, the quality of those contributions tends to be of low value, since there will be a few employees who will contribute like crazy while others will not. Those who do not contribute as readily tend to be those who guard their content more closely and do not contribute anything of any great value.

While the carrot and stick approach may be useful in getting employees excited about a new corporate initiative, for any long-term success, you will need to incorporate the repository into the business process; hence, the process approach.

Each business process should be defined and carried out in accordance with the approved process. Hopefully those processes have been optimized through some form of business process analysis. It would then be fairly easy to append onto the process a new step of copying and registering key documents into a repository.

That east coast IT firm did eventually update some of their defined processes to further facilitate the capture of content. They chose selected key processes, such as the client engagement proposals, which followed a defined process of proposal development. At the end of that proposal development process, new steps were incorporated to ensure that the proposal and related supporting documents were properly captured in a proposal repository. Capturing that content, consistently and repeatedly, later proved to be of great value in terms of content reuse.

With either approach, it is important to quantify knowledge

sharing. Quantifying the sharing will allow management to assess the success of the organization's sharing or the lack thereof.

知

There are other ways in which you can prospect for knowledge, both within the enterprise and externally. Besides relying on employees to contribute their content, you can actively seek out that content and automatically populate a repository.

If your organization utilizes a document management system or even a simple file system on a shared server, you have the opportunity to access those files. Remember that every organization serious about productivity should have a document management system. There are no excuses for not utilizing this basic tool.

There are many products available that will allow you to define a number of file directories and have the product automatically scan those directories for newly added or changed files. Once tagged as new or changed, they can be copied into an actively managed repository. The challenge with this method is to properly index those documents. While there are automatic indexing tools available, they all have limited use due to their relatively high error rate. A better approach would be to utilize the metadata entered by the author within the application; e.g., entering metadata within Microsoft Word by using the Properties Summary to enter author name, an abstract, and key words.

As long as you have access to the files, it is possible to copy them into a repository. For the most part, the only time you won't have this option is for locally stored files, such as those on each employee's hard disk drive. Unfortunately, this is where most individuals store their content; and as stated earlier, this practice should not be tolerated by any organization.

External content can also be captured through the use of Internet-based tools often called *spiders*. A spider crawls a web site and copies all or selected content into your repository. Many organizations point their crawler to their competitor's web site, thus getting near real-time information on posted changes, such as new press releases. Obviously this has limited use given the highly controlled nature of web content on corporate web sites. Nevertheless, it is yet another tool that you can utilize to capture content.

知

There are other occasions during which organizations actively prospect for knowledge. One of the most popular times is just prior to loosing a valuable employee, either through retirement, transfer, or termination.

Given the immense value in that employee's mind—their institutional knowledge—many firms offer employees an incentive to share that knowledge before they go. This is often performed by a recorded interview of the employee. This interview, whether or not it is videotaped, is referred to as *knowledge harvesting.*

Digitizing and storing the videotape is of limited value unless one has a level of granularity needed to quickly find the information for which they are seeking. A 20-hour tape would otherwise take 20 hours to view, which is virtually useless in today's hectic business environment. The way to solve this is to transcribe the interview word for word, thus providing a means to adequately search the content. When a hit is found, the application could provide a short synopsis of the surrounding text, or jump directly to the video segment that relates to the hit.

Another approach, which may be performed in parallel with the video recording, is to inventory the employee's content with him or her, seeking guidance in adding metadata and applying context to selected documents. This documented information would then be considerably more useful, due to its qualities of being easily searchable and sharable.

Another time in which an organization may want to capture content is for some high value, repeatable, decision making processes. It may be worth the investment to track and document this decision making process.

For example, technicians fix equipment in the field. Fixing such equipment is a repeatable process, and having support engineers or other technicians working in the field is relatively expensive. Any small savings in their time would add up to significant cost savings in labor and travel costs. While every equipment manufacturer has repair manuals, any good field engineer has their own set of notes upon which they rely much more so than the published manuals. As you can imagine, the value of these notes is high. Collecting these notes from the various field engineers and assembling them into a collective document that all technicians could use would result in a very high-value knowledge sharing initiative.

In your organization, think about what institutional knowledge exists in the employees' minds and, likewise, what critical information exists in the tangible content of those employees. Their documents, e-mail, and even scraps of paper in notepads may turn out to be much more valuable than the new programmer who submitted every document he could in order to be eligible for that free trip to Phoenix.

知

Employees' collective knowledge is an organization's most valuable resource, yet we spend a great deal of time prospecting for that knowledge and its byproduct - information. A small and nimble organization thus tends to be better adapted at harnessing that knowledge, while large organizations can only benefit from that collective knowledge if they overtly harness it. In order to do so, the large organization must proactively encourage knowledge sharing. Sharing such knowledge and related quantifiable content, such as white papers; reports; briefings; etc., all require an organization with a high *organizational IQ*. The more mature an organization, the more sharing and reuse of content and employee knowledge.

One way to start a knowledge prospecting effort is to perform a *knowledge audit*. A knowledge audit will reveal what knowledge the organization has, how it flows, what the obstacles to sharing and collaboration may be, and what technology and infrastructure exist to enable such knowledge sharing. The knowledge audit will likely focus on processes and information flows just as much as documenting what knowledge currently exists in the organization.

The knowledge audit may take a macro level view, which focuses on high-level repositories, flows, and general cultural attitudes within the organization. A more detailed audit may also be performed, which would analyze the specific knowledge and content assets, information flows, and bottlenecks.

Once the audit has been performed, with its findings reported to management, the knowledge prospecting team will have a much better understanding of their project's scope and the challenges that lay ahead.

Not sharing the collective knowledge that exists is lost knowledge, and lost knowledge is squandered capital.

Section Two

Collaboration, Culture, and Processes

"Perception is reality."

— *Anonymous*

Chapter Nine

Collaboration— It's a Funny Thing

The funny thing about collaboration is that everyone says that they value and respect teamwork and collaboration, but few organizations promote it.

Many of us perform collaboration to some degree, but we are guarded in how much information we share and knowledge we impart to others. Employees, especially *knowledge workers* (a general term referring to white-collar employees who utilize their tacit knowledge along with enterprise information to make decisions), are retained for their expertise and intellectual value. Parting with our information and knowledge, therefore, is a double-edged sword. We have to communicate and contribute to the work processes and associated teams, yet we want to ensure that we will remain valuable over the long term.

There are several ways in which employees collaborate, ranging from contributing to a team that has a unified goal, to sharing content with those in the organization who have a need for it. Another form of collaboration is the enabling of employees to efficiently communicate and share individual inputs. This form of collaboration can benefit from the enabling technologies that aid such communications.

However, in today's globalized business environment in which workers are often knowledge-centric mobile workers who function in an extended business-to-business community comprised of partners, suppliers, and consultants, the need to effectively collaborate has now become a business necessity. Collaboration improves cycle times of innovation, allowing one to bring products to market quicker and operate more effectively.

The reuse of content, along with collaboration, is what achieving the competitive advantage is all about in today's modern enterprise. Collaboration allows us to work across organizational boundaries to achieve strategic organizational goals. It allows us to better communicate, discuss, review, and approve ideas and work-products in a more efficient manner.

The remainder of this chapter will briefly cover the challenges of collaboration, followed by a focus on the enabling technologies that support collaboration.

知

In order to achieve even a modest increase in collaboration between employees, the culture of the organization must be supportive. Trust, simply put, is a requirement for collaboration.

Most organizations still value and reward individual achievement, and this is understandable. We are generally judged on our perceived value (for perception is reality) and on our recent accomplishments. All organizations are like this, to some extent. There are extremes, however, in which collaboration flourishes or is lifeless.

An adversarial and competition-oriented organization offers little real hope of promoting collaboration and teamwork, and is at a high-risk for failing any knowledge management implementation. Employees must also not feel as though collaborating will lessen their own value, status, or job security.

Therefore assessing the culture of the organization is important prior to any system deployment. This is often a function of the knowledge audit, described in the previous chapter. The knowledge audit focuses not only on existing knowledge and related content, but also on the flow of knowledge between employees. This flow, or lack thereof, is often a direct correlation to the organization's true culture.

The probability of acceptance for any system that promotes collaboration is an important finding that should be conveyed to management and discussed. Some organizations thrive on teamwork and will, therefore, welcome any new system that increases productivity. Other organizations, however, are adversarial and tend to hoard content, thus offering a real challenge for any IT practitioner.

As you perform the knowledge audit, assess the hoarding versus sharing of content. The organization that allows hoarding will be the high-risk implementation. There are always exceptions, however, for every organization has a mix of people, some of whom are natural hoarders, while others are not. Recognize the exceptions and focus on the overall culture.

Changing the culture will be difficult, if not impossible. Either way, changing the culture will likely be out of scope for any IT project. Those who do take on the culture will find themselves in for a real challenge.

I worked for two major insurance companies which had similar business models and practices, yet very different cultures. As you can probably guess, one system was implemented successfully while the other was a much greater challenge.

These two firms were similar in many ways. They both issued insurance policies and handled claims. They were in a highly regulated industry, with similar processes.

The first firm, located in Baltimore, Maryland, was an old and venerable insurance company with a successful history. This firm, however, had procedures that dated back a decade or so, and its employees tended to be in their 40's and 50's. While they relied on automated IT systems, they accepted them with some reluctance. I also noticed that many employees tended to view their IT department as disruptive to their daily work, and treated those IT staffers as second-class employees who were employed only to serve them.

My project in Baltimore was to implement a true collaboration system. The objective was to improve productivity of claims and related lawsuits by improving the content and knowledge sharing between the various employees who contributed to the acceptance or rejection of a claim.

The challenges for my team stared immediately. We had employees who were openly hostile to any change in their work processes. Some kept their notes on paper and refused to enter the information into any system, citing everything from "I don't have time" to "that's stupid" to "I have carpal tunnel syndrome."

As you can guess, the Baltimore system was a headache for everyone: the employees; our client; and us. We tried our best, but the culture was ingrained and against us. While the system was deployed, it was never very successful and did not live up to its capability.

A similar insurance company in Florida, however, was relatively new to the industry and had grown rapidly over the prior five years. Their employees were generally young and had good working and social relationships with their IT department. It was a fun place to work and a fun place for my team to visit.

The knowledge audit and subsequent requirements definition task was simple to complete. Everyone was helpful and looked forward to the new system which we would soon deliver. Sure enough, the system was deployed with ease, training went quicker than expected, and everyone from the CIO down to a policy adjuster thought the project was a great success.

Productivity continued to rise, and the firm continues to grow (the Baltimore company has now ceased to exist).

知

This chapter has thus far focused on the social and cultural aspects of collaboration. As you can tell from the two insurance companies, the culture of the organization has a great deal of influence on the probability of success for any collaboration system.

Now, however, let's examine the technical capabilities that collaboration systems can support, and discuss supporting modern workgroups through collaboration.

Employees today are just as likely to work in distant offices, at client sites, or telecommute as they are to work in a large corporate office building with many colleagues and extensive on-site support staff resources. Getting these mobile workers the access to repositories and timely information that they need to be productive is vital.

Fortunately, collaborative tools exist in abundance. When the tools are combined with secure dial-in access to corporate repositories, they offer the employee similar productivity capability to those who are physically at the corporate office.

In many organizations, e-mail has become the collaborative tool of choice. E-mail, however, is being pushed to perform many functions for which it was never intended. Long e-mail chains, with upwards of 20 e-mails appended together, are disorganized and put a terrible strain on the corporate e-mail infrastructure. Modern peer-to-peer technologies and related tools offer a much more effective way to collaborate. Tools that help facilitate collaboration, and compliment e-mail, include:

- Electronic Whiteboard—The electronic whiteboard is similar to the standard office whiteboard with which we are all familiar. The difference is that this whiteboard is on the computer monitor. You can draw or type in the whiteboard window and have the contents displayed on the monitors of others, regardless of their location. This allows for everyone to share the brainstorming capability of a whiteboard, even at distant locations. Other whiteboards offer a radio-frequency detector that physically broadcasts content from a real office whiteboard. The radio-frequency mechanism tracks writing and erasing of real whiteboard pens and broadcasts the content to the monitors of those who are not in the room. This allows one group of users to use a real whiteboard and "conference-in" others.
- Instant Messaging (IM)—Instant messaging has evolved from chat capability used by teenagers on America Online to a business enabling technology. Instant messaging allows for multiple people to "chat" within one shared computer window. This allows disparate groups to discuss or otherwise brainstorm ideas and conduct on-line meetings.

- Threaded Discussion—Similar to instant messaging in that the text of each participant is appended onto the scrolling text of a message or discussion, threaded discussions allow for the ongoing discussion concerning a selected topic. The text of one participant is added to the text of others, thus creating a date-and-time descending list. This can be useful for long-term discussions over a period of time, such as when a topic is discussed over several months.
- Desktop Video Teleconferencing—Video teleconferencing (VTC) is a powerful capability for physically distant staff, and is now available directly on a user's desktop. The cost of desktop VTCs is very low today and the quality and capability is high. The only limiting factor is bandwidth; the more the better. Every enterprise with distant staff should implement desktop VTC. It is a cheap and powerful capability that offers substantial productivity potential.
- Shared Desktop—First used by computer technicians to help them remotely troubleshoot a user's desktop, the shared desktop offers the ability to jointly view computer windows, usually as the entire computer monitor. This is especially useful for those who need hands-on training on a new application or otherwise need to be "talked through" various steps on their screen.
- Shared Workspaces—Similar to the shared desktop, the workspace is a shared application, such as a document authoring tool that can be used by multiple people. The "workspace" could be any sort of application, but is typically a file repository or a document-centric application used for joint authoring.

Collaboration, therefore, involves the all-important social and cultural issues that may be barriers to high productivity, and the technology enabling collaborative tools that greatly assist the knowledge worker. There is, however, much more to collaboration than what is covered in this one chapter. True collaboration is only attainable from the sum of all of the contents of this book. Collaboration requires the delivery of content to the right person at the right time; only then can one turn intellectual property into working capital.

"Let him, that would move the world, first move himself."

— Socrates (469-399 BC)
Greek philosopher

Chapter Ten

The Great Impediment: Cultural Acceptance

The lack of cultural acceptance during many system implementations is worthy of the title, "The Great Impediment," for cultural issues have a far greater probability of derailing a system than any other reason.

As noted throughout this book, there is a lot that can go wrong with a system implementation; hence the need for a good project manager to be paranoid. Topping the list of challenges is managing the end-user acceptance, and the greatest impediment to end-user acceptance is culture clash. If the organization's culture is inherently at odds with the changes brought on by the new system, then the probability of success is dismal.

I experienced the difficulties of cultural acceptance during one of my first content and collaboration projects. The system, which was for a financial organization in Virginia, was fairly simple, yet it offered substantial productivity improvement for the entire organization. Technically, everything went smoothly, and neither funding nor senior management caused problems. It should have been a simple implementation, but it was not. The challenges we faced upon deployment included:

- Resistance to change—There are those who simply do not want change. The "I have been doing it this way for five years, why do I need to change?" argument is hard for an outsider to overcome. Therefore the importance of the organization's management to not only support the initiative, but to actively participate in the project, is critical to reducing risk.
- Resistance in sharing content—Our content, and especially our knowledge, is intimate; we don't regularly share it with others unless we know how it will be used. Some employees resist entering their content into "some new system" that they neither fully understand nor trust.
- Resistance by middle management—Middle management can be a problem. They tend to have the most to lose in regards to their "control" of how the organization operates. Middle management controls content and work processes in a mostly manual organization; that is the majority of their daily job. However a new system will often be seen as a direct threat to that job, and thus will be resisted.
- Lies—There are those who simply do not want the new system. They will say and do anything to prevent it from "taking over." Regarding that financial organization in Virginia, along with the deployment of the new system, we upgraded much of their hardware, including end-user desktops and monitors, giving them much larger, crisper monitors. One employee, who was a problem from the beginning, objected to the new system on her desk to the point of simply refusing to use it. Her argument was that the system was emitting radiation from the new monitor and was giving her a headache. Even after replacing the monitor with several unrelated models, she continued to be a constant complainer, until she left (rumor had it that she left on long-term disability leave).

Is there any way to deal with someone who leaves the office complaining of headaches? Probably not. There's one in every crowd....

Other than those headache-prone employees, how should one minimize the risk of cultural acceptance? There are steps that you can take to minimize this issue.

In general, IT professionals tend to focus far too much time on the middle phases of a project life cycle. We spend a great deal of time designing the system and the user-interface, and integrating it with legacy applications. We perform the requirements analysis at the beginning, and at the end we perform training. However, ensuring cultural acceptance or cultural harmony for a new system requires much more.

An ounce of prevention is greater than a pound of cure, so the saying goes. Therefore commit to spending quality time at both ends of the project life cycle by:

- Spending some time getting to know the organization as a whole at the beginning of the project, before the formal requirements definition phase. Gather and analyze data regarding the organization's mission, objective, constraints, budget, and customers, and get to know who the real decision-makers are. This activity is called the cultural audit.
- Listening to users—really listen.
- Communicating the new system's purpose and how it will improve their individual daily work experience.
- Obtaining user acceptance by working with them from the beginning and keeping them informed throughout the project.
- Performing the knowledge audit (described in the preceding chapters) and focusing on the cultural aspects of the organization.
- Keeping senior management involved in the project, and having them articulate its status and importance to their employees.
- Paying special attention to middle management and understanding their need for control. Communicate how the new system will enhance their decision-making and will allow them to focus on the more critical decisions and overall control of the organization.

- Focusing on training and support near the end of the project. One-on-one support is often all that is needed to make an employee feel that they are important and that you care about their needs and happiness with the new system.

As you can tell from this list, good social skills are needed to successfully obtain results. For that reason, a "business analyst" team member is often important to communicate with users and management. The business analyst typically has good social skills and is a good listener.

Overcoming the cultural barriers is paramount. You may be lucky and not encounter such stiff resistance, but inevitably you will find this in some organizations. On all my projects, I personally plan on taking that extra time to understand and manage the culture. If it turns out that the time is not fully needed, I modify the project's schedule appropriately and count myself lucky.

"Never mistake motion for action."

— *Ernest Hemingway (1899-1961)*

Chapter Eleven

Work Process Automation

Automating the processes of each community of practice is essential for enterprise optimization and represents one of the four pillars of Knowledge Nirvana.

Processes are the series of actions or functions that are performed to complete an operation. We live by processes, at work and at home.

Each of us start a process every morning when we wake up. We brush our teeth, eat breakfast, drink coffee, and maybe read the morning newspaper. This "Pre Go to Work" process, as we can label it, may deviate on occasion, but in general it is a fairly routine process for you that can be defined, modeled, and documented.

All processes, even the "Pre Go to Work" process, are comprised of actions, inputs, outputs, and dependencies. We have a dependency on our newspaper carrier to deliver our newspapers prior to our retrieving them from our front yard (or in my case, from underneath the car).

Most every process can be further broken down into many subprocesses. The "Pre Go to Work" process is comprised of a subprocess that we can call "Drinking Coffee." That sub-process itself can be further broken into two additional sub-processes, those of "Prepare Coffee" and "Drink Coffee."

"Prepare Coffee" has inputs of ground coffee, water, and a coffee filter. The output is coffee to drink. This requires a preparer (probably you) and a coffee maker. Factors influencing the process include your diet plan and the availability of ground coffee.

One can model all these processes in great detail and drill down into all the various levels of sub-processes, which may seem never-ending. For this reason, you have two key decisions to make prior to modeling a process.

The first decision is to define what process you actually wish to model. What this really comes down to is determining what the boundaries of that process are that you are interested in. In our "Pre Go to Work" process, we are only interested in the activities prior to going to work in the morning. We are not interested in how the coffee got to the store or who purchased the coffee. We have, there-fore, made an overt decision concerning the boundaries of the process.

Secondly, you need to define how deep into the process you are going to model; i.e., how far are you going to drill down in each process? In our example, "Prepare Coffee" is the lowest level sub-process in which we are interested.

Now we have defined our process and determined to what level we need to model the sub-processes. Defining the process to model should be based on a business decision concerning which process you are preparing to automate. How far to drill down is often a fairly subjective decision. Take your best guess based upon what you know of the process thus far, but be prepared to drill down further as necessary.

知

In the example above, I referred to modeling of the processes, which include defining the inputs, outputs, dependencies, etc. This is further discussed in chapter twelve, *Process Improvement*. Let's leave the modeling detail for later and focus now on the key aspect of this chapter: automating the processes.

The reason to automate a process should be obvious. Automating the process of a workgroup can significantly compress time and effort for everyone affected in the community of practice.

You eliminate the time lag in the process while improving control over the process. The speed of the process can increase, and thus the efficiency of those in the workgroup rises, often dramatically with a properly implemented solution.

Think about the average non-automated process. It is most likely sequential in nature. That means step one gets completed, then it goes on to step two, and so forth. The majority of time in the process, however, is idle time. It may only take two minuets to review and approve a routine purchase order (PO), but it may take three days for interoffice mail to deliver it to the appropriate reviewer, at which point it will probably sit on their desk for two more days prior to the reviewer taking any action. If that reviewer is on vacation for two weeks, the PO will most likely sit on that desk for two weeks.

All this can and should dramatically change in any organization that is serious about optimizing their key resources, employees, and content. The time lag to deliver the PO is all but eliminated in an automated workflow. The workflow can also add intelligent routing capability that currently does not exist in the manual process. That PO does not have to sit on the vacationing reviewer's desk for two weeks if the enterprise has a pre-defined business rule that automatically routes the PO to an authorized supervisor who is available.

Not all processes can be effectively automated, however. The "Pre Go to Work" process is not high on my list of processes to automate for several reasons. Firstly, it does not utilize a great deal of content that can be automated. Secondly, it does not involve many individuals in a workgroup; therefore, the information flow is limited. Finally, that process is not a high value process. Even if I could automate it, it would have minimal impact on overall productivity.

What can effectively be automated are those processes that are highly dependent upon content and involve many individuals in a workgroup, also called a community of practice (see chapter seven). A PO for office supplies, for example, is comprised almost entirely of content. It is then routed through a process that includes approvals, purchasing, and finance, all of which can be easily automated.

Note that your existing processes, automated or not, may either be well defined or rather informal. A well-defined process may exist for a PO. For example, every PO over $2,000 must receive a second authorized signature. This *business rule* has been established and the PO itself is merely the container for this action. Many processes, however, are not well defined or have been altered over time, posing more of a challenge to anyone automating that work process.

知

Automating processes can be achieved by a number of means. The most popular are commercially available workflow software products, which may either be applications or tools for developers. Workflow software automates the process and operates with standard applications, such as your organization's financial system, employee e-mail, and word processing applications.

The PO, for example, may be comprised of an Excel spreadsheet or a specific forms document (an e-form), which is then attached to the workflow process. The process for approving the PO is predefined. It starts with a requester who initially fills out the PO and initiates the workflow. The workflow application knows who the initiator is (by their user name and password), recognizes who the appropriate supervisor is, and automatically routes the workflow to that person. At the supervisory level, it can be electronically approved by clicking an "approve" button in the workflow application, at which time the PO would move to the next step in the process, such as purchasing.

This PO example is very simple. By no means does it represent the capabilities or limitations of modern workflow products that offer complex conditional routing. The PO approval workflow, for example, can be programmed to extract the dollar amount of the PO and automatically route the workflow to the second approving manager, if that PO value is over a $2,000 threshold. Furthermore, the routing may be sequential, parallel, or conditional. The PO may be sent to two approving managers in parallel, and only upon both of their approvals (the condition) is it then routed to purchasing.

Much in a workgroup can be automated. You only need to define the requirements, select the appropriate workflow product that meets the requirements, and then customize and integrate the workflow product into your enterprise. That sounds like a lot of work, and it can be. However you generally only need to perform this effort once per process. Once developed, let the workgroup utilize this new automated process which allows them to significantly improve their productivity.

知

Most IT professionals divide workflow products into two general categories: production workflow and ad hoc workflow.

In production workflow, think of a structured assembly line of information flow. The PO approval is an assembly line workflow that follows business rules that are probably well defined.

Another example of a production, or structured, workflow is an insurance claim. Upon receiving the claim, the insurance company determines what type of claim it is and then routes the claim to the appropriate department, such as auto casualty for the southeast states.

Once in the Southeast Auto Casualty Department, the claim undergoes a structured review by various workgroup employees. These employees make determinations relating to the claim. Each determination, along with related notes, can easily be captured in a database field or in a Word document. This information is then assembled into an electronic case folder (similar in concept to a manila paper folder) and managed by the workflow application.

Not all workflows, however, are so structured. Let's say you drafted a new policy document for your department and now want a number of people to review it. You could set up an ad hoc workflow at that time to automate the review of that draft document.

Key to ad hoc, or unstructured workflow, is that it must be very easy to use. Many non-IT users will need to intuitively set up their own workflows at any given time.

If you find that you are using the draft policy review workflow on a regular basis, it should be fairly easy to reuse that workflow repeatedly. It may be shared with others in your community of practice, or even formalized as a standard workflow for the enterprise. The key to any good workflow product is flexibility.

知

There are workflow applications and tools made specifically for automating processes. However, there are other means of automating a process, such as e-mail and groupware applications.

E-mail can also offer workflow capability. How many of us have sent content in an e-mail body or as an attached file for others to review? Probably all of us. Is this not an automated workflow? Absolutely. It is just not quite as elegant and does not have all the functionality and features found in workflow-specific products.

Many e-mail applications do allow you to establish simple scripts with if-then rules. This works nicely for many simple workflows.

Groupware offers workflow capabilities similar to e-mail, but usually adds additional functionality, such as the ability to establish more complex conditional rules.

For simple ad hoc workflows, e-mail and groupware can work very well. There are, however, significant limitations to e-mail and groupware which need to be understood. Most importantly, they are not real workflow products. Any enterprise serious about productivity and content management must leverage workflow to its fullest extent and, therefore, should utilize the efficiency of a real workflow product.

知

It is hard to describe all the possible functions and features of a workflow product, for they are many and they differ for each individual product. What is important is that you select one that meets your requirements and is flexible.

The ability to add attachments, such as a Word document or an Excel file, to the process is common to all workflow products. Complex conditional formulas, sequential and parallel routing, and the ability to add digital signatures or other means of authentication are also common.

What is not necessarily common is the ability to manage a single workflow over multiple workflow servers, which may be a requirement for a geographically dispersed community of practice.

For example, if you are in the New York office, yet are part of a cross-functional team that includes coworkers in Chicago and Atlanta, you probably have workflow servers in New York, Chicago, and Atlanta. Managing a single workflow process, even a simple PO approval process, over these distinct servers can be technically difficult. Some workflow applications will attempt to do this by having three disparate workflows, using the example above, and then append them together. However you lose most of the status and management functionality of the workflow, which is often unacceptable.

知

In general, there is a trade-off between overall capability and what you get "out of the box" with each workflow product. An easy to use product may offer a great deal of pre-defined functionality out of the box, but may not allow the IT staff the ability to develop highly customized workflows at a later date. Like everything in life, it all comes down to a trade off in capabilities and cost.

This is why I initially started this chapter by referring to workflow "applications and tools." Workflow applications tend to be the pre-defined and easy to use workflows, while workflow tools allow the IT staff to develop highly customized workflows. The significant downside—the trade-off—with the tools is that they come with almost nothing out of the box; i.e., they require significant programming to get them to do anything. So even automating a simple PO approval workflow requires a significant undertaking. Again, it is a trade off.

Obviously the distinction between workflow applications and workflow tools is subjective. Most workflow product vendors will argue that their product offers flexibility with all the functionality and features anyone would need.

知

All mature workflow tools, and even many workflow applications, are comprised of three major functional modules: the workflow engine; the process designer; and a status control and monitoring module.

The workflow engine is the software code that is at the heart of the program. It controls the workflows, the routing scenarios, the file attachments, and much more.

The process designer is a builder tool used to create each workflow. While it may be text-based, it more likely is graphical in nature and comprised of objects that represent sub-processes. Clicking on a sub-process graphical icon, for example, may visually explode that process and show its sub-processes on a visual map. In a production workflow, all this can become complex. Therefore the graphical object-oriented nature of the workflow designer with a visual map becomes crucial to maintaining one's sanity.

Finally, the status control and monitoring module provides individual users and management with information regarding the workflows.

The status control and monitoring functions are also critical to maintaining control over the workflows. Monitoring may be *pull* or *push* in nature. A user may pull (query and retrieve) the data associated with the workflow status, or the product may be pre-programmed to push the status automatically to one or more users when a condition occurs.

An example of the usefulness of the push mode is a user who is in the middle of a workflow, but has not acted upon the workflow for 48 hours. This delay would obviously affect the efficiency of the workflow, and the initiators may want to be notified so they can take action.

All status information is stored in a database and is available for statistical analysis or auditing purposes. If the workgroup is highly automated, and hence uses workflow extensively, there is likely to be some very interesting data associated with the performance of each employee. This data is now readily available for management's review.

The benefit to this is that management not only knows the performance statistics of many employees, but also knows the real-time status of actions. Knowing how many insurance claims are in what phase of the process, all in real-time, is valuable to management.

The downside is the potential for the "big-brother" syndrome, in which employees become paranoid that management knows what they are doing and is constantly looking over their shoulders, although in this case, doing so electronically and very efficiently!

It is not uncommon for workflow vendors to offer a version of their product, usually oriented to the European marketplace, which greatly limits status reporting and statistical analysis to comply with European labor laws.

知

Hemingway's "Never mistake motion for action" observation is valid in workflow automation. A process may encompass a lot of motion, but that doesn't ensure an efficient action.

Automating a workgroup's process with a workflow product should offer significant improvements in productivity. Unfortunately, this may simply speed up an otherwise inefficient process. This is shameful, and does not contribute to our goal of achieving dramatic improvements in productivity in an effort to achieve a competitive advantage for the organization.

As we model our processes, creating the "as-is" model, we need to keep a keen eye on improving the process, not just improving the speed of the process. This key effort, which is filled with perils, is the subject of the next chapter, *Process Improvement*.

"It is not the strongest of the species that survive, nor the most intelligent, but the one most responsive to change."

— *Charles Darwin*

Chapter Twelve

Process Improvement

Previous chapters discussed process automation, also known as workflow. Automated workflow is an extremely powerful technology, but should one automate inefficient and, most likely, out-of-date processes? Hopefully not.

Before you implement any workflow application, you must consider to what extent you wish to improve upon the processes you are about to automate. This is called process improvement, and is also often called business process reengineering (BPR).

Let's look at a simple example.

One of my clients, a nation-wide insurance company, had to install and integrate into their mission critical process a new integrated document management (IDM) system. This system comprised imaging, document management, records management, and workflow functionality, along with access to various structured data.

Senior management at that company wanted to install the new system and had worked the project into their budget cycle. It was not, therefore, a hard sell to get them to agree to the recommendations given to them regarding the system components. However, upon conducting the requirements analysis, which focused on interviewing the line staff personnel for the majority of the functional requirements, it became obvious that many of their official processes were out-of-date with their current work processes (the way they really do business).

This is because the processes had evolved over time, with and without management's consent.

Furthermore, and just as important, we all realized that a new system based on their functional requirements alone would alter some of their current processes. Clearly, the processes were going to change, so the automated workflow needed to change at some level, whether management liked that or not.

Before going on with how to conduct process improvement, let's spend a little time examining how processes change.

Back to the insurance company example, the processes changed over time, which is common. Changes occur due to personnel leaving, staff out on maternity leave, promotions, or any number of other reasons. The point is that they change. The employees in the organization adapt to these changes with, and sometimes without, management's knowledge.

Processes also change, or more likely adapt, to new automated systems that do not quite fit to their existing processes.

The second primary reason why processes will change with any new IT system is that some steps can be completely automated, thus removing the employee directly from the process.

Let's say one step in the well defined and management-approved process has an employee performing a certain function. With a new IT system, that function goes away, thus completely eliminating that employee from the process. This streamlines the process and likely improves organizational productivity.

Again, it is important to remember that processes will change with or without management's blessing. You must, therefore, take this into consideration.

I once reviewed a process that I did not much care for with a group of corporate management. When I suggested a change, I got shot down quickly. I firmly believed, however, that times had changed and the current process in question was antiquated and needed refinement.

When discussing the process with one senior manager, I asked why it should be done a certain way.

The reply was a classic. He said, "because that is the we have been doing it for the last 15 years."

Enough said.

知

Now you have come to the inevitable conclusion that you must perform some process improvement activities in order to implement your new application and ensure the return on investment (ROI) that management expects. Here comes the big question: how much process improvement are you willing to perform?

Do you make minor improvements here and there that are non-controversial, but yet will probably not dramatically improve the organization's productivity? Or do you attempt to implement radical changes that will likely ensure a high ROI for the solution? Are you and management prepared for significant resistance?

That's a tough decision to make.

If the process has been highly adaptive to changing office requirements, personnel, and automated systems, chances are great that the process is significantly inefficient and out-of-date.

To conduct a real process improvement effort is a test of management's resolve and employee willingness to accept change gracefully. Change, however, is something that most of us naturally dislike.

So here are the two primary approaches to process improvement.

On one side of the spectrum is the simple process improvement effort that focuses on changing those steps in the process that are obvious and that most employees can agree upon. Think of this as a refinement of the process. It is evolutionary and not revolutionary, and looks for incremental improvements. This is often called *process improvement*, which generally connotes the gentler approach.

Business process reengineering (BPR) is on the other side of the spectrum from process improvement. It is revolutionary, not evolutionary. It tends to be a fairly radical approach of significant change to the current process. BPR efforts seek widespread and significant improvements.

BPR can be described as taking an eraser to a white board that depicts the current process. You erase the current process and start all over, defining the various steps in an optimized process, regardless of what the duties and assignments of employees currently are. Now you can see why this is called radical.

BPR is very difficult to perform successfully. Some believe it is impossible to succeed on any real enterprise-wide scale. It does, however, offer the organization the most to gain.

BPR is emotional. When people think of BPR, they often associate it with head-count reduction; i.e., layoffs. Even if no staff reduction occurs, you will significantly alter job functions, with some employees gaining responsibilities while others lose responsibilities, influence, and power.

For these reasons, BPR has fallen out of favor. With this radical approach, it is difficult to achieve success; it is time consuming; and it upsets the workforce. Yet it can, and does, work.

知

How to Perform Process Improvement. Functionally it sounds so simple. You create a process map, a map of the current "as-is" process, either on paper or through an automated tool such as Visio. This process map is often a block diagram that shows each sub-process, breaking it down into inputs, outputs, value created, resources required (per the sub-process), and its interaction with other sub-processes.

There are a number of popular modeling methodologies with diagramming techniques that have stood the test of time. One of the most popular is the IDEF family of models. IDEF was originally developed for the U.S. Air Force to graphically depict diagrams for complex change management projects. The IDEF0 model is designed to show decisions, actions, and related activities of an organization or system. In the IDEF0 diagram, the function of the sub-task is depicted inside a box. To the left of the box are the inputs to that task, to the right are the outputs. Coming in from the top of the box are "controls" to the task, and coming into the box from below are "mechanisms."

Besides the popular IDEF0 model, which focuses on processes, and is therefore of the most value for process improvement activities, the IDEF1 model is often used for information modeling. There are other IDEF models available, and then there are those who dislike IDEF models completely and use one of the many other models.

As you can probably tell by now, there is a lot to these models. It can be a complex effort just to try to understand, let alone master, all of the popular methodologies, diagramming techniques, and automated tools.

Fortunately there is a lot of good information on the Internet and through books focusing on change management that go into greater detail, if you so desire.

What is important now is for you to decide on what it is you are going to model and how you are going to model it. A real methodology may only be required for larger, more formal, projects.

If you are just starting out, try a simple IDEF0 model focusing on processes, and use Visio or one of the many IDEF0 specific modeling tools available today.

Once the process map is complete, you must analyze the process and determine which areas should be changed. Document this in the "to-be" process model. This "to-be" model depicts the process as it should be after it has been optimized and otherwise changed by the project.

Present your new "to-be" process model to management for approval, then go implement the change. Simple, right?

Let's look at the problems you will likely encounter throughout the modeling process, management review, and implementation, even in the best of circumstances. I call these *process landmines*— the landmines that, when you hit one unexpectedly, can kill your project.

Conflicting Information

The first thing you will likely encounter as you define the "as-is" process model is conflicting information from employees. One manager, for example, claims they do it one way, while another insists it is really done another way. Who is right? At first it will be hard to tell, since everyone will insist that their way is the correct way.

It is time for you to play detective. You will have to be a Sherlock Holmes, not an Inspector Clouseau, to determine which process is correct. You will also need the people skills to deal with all individuals involved. Determining the current process is not too hard to ascertain, yet it is time-consuming; hence the long hours of consulting time often required to achieve a fairly accurate "as-is" model.

Another common problem—really a deviation from the above—is that everyone you interview for the "as-is" model is correct. They are all correct, that is, because they all use different processes. This often happens when there is one approved process that has been adapted to a changing environment in more than one location, whether it is multiple offices or even multiple departments in the same division.

Your challenge now is to determine how to break this startling discovery to management—that each section/office/unit has their own processes, which is probably unlike what management told you when they commissioned you for this project. In my experience, denial is the most common reaction by management when presented with such facts.

The silver lining on this situation, however, is that you have the opportunity to examine several similar processes and select the best ideas from them for your "to-be" process model. So once you get over the management issue, you really have a lot more data to draw upon—several real-world "as-is" models as opposed to only one.

Approved Process Deviation

Let's say the organization for which you are performing the analysis has a defined process that everyone is to follow. The process has been approved by senior management and must be followed. The problem is that the process is not followed.

Guess what? You are the one who must tell management that their employees are not following the process, and shame on management for not knowing this. Are you really going to tell them that? Hopefully you have a long-term contract signed, for I have seen real cases of management pulling the plug on process improvement projects because of their embarrassment over what you have uncovered.

One thing is certain, though. When you find such deviations, it is important that you present these findings to management at some point. The reason is two-fold. First, and most importantly, implementing a new IT system will be more complex given the deviations in the process, and will, therefore, take longer and cost more than originally anticipated. Remember that management must approve your invoices for payment.

The second reason is that, when presented correctly (politically correctly, that is), it shows management that you are performing a real value for your fee.

Only Listen to Me

This is a classic problem with process improvement or any related requirements analysis task.

Your task is to define the processes of an office. The kick-off meeting went well, all the employees seem nice and friendly, and you are starting to think that this project may run ahead of schedule.

Then you show up for the first process improvement meeting and find that only the office manager is there from the client's organization. The office manager informs you that the employees are too busy with their day-to-day responsibilities and that he is qualified to provide you with all the information regarding the processes. In essence, only listen to me.

This is the kiss of death for any process improvement project. To succeed one must interview as many people and as many types of employees as possible that relate to the process in question.

Interview everyone, if that is practical. Do not rely on just one or two people for input, especially if they are from management.

There is an old saying that goes something like this: "The day you become a manager is the last day you really know what is going on." There is a lot of truth to that. I know, because I have performed many process improvement projects over the years and have found that I get the least amount of accurate information from managers (besides, I have been just such a manager myself).

In fact, I usually just rely on managers for the big-picture issues, macro-level requirements, and to approve my findings. The details of a process I get from the lowest level line employee; i.e., the "hands-on" employee.

The Power Grab

When an organization is undertaking a process improvement project, most employees know there will be at least some changes. There are those who will utilize this change for their personal gain; i.e., the power grab.

I am not going to discuss this in any detail or share any examples of the power grab, for it is fairly self-explanatory. Do be aware of it, however. Whether you are an in-house IT employee or an external consultant, you have the fiduciary duty to create the most optimal "to-be" processes that you can. You cannot do this if employees influence your recommendations for their personal gain.

Illegal Activities

It is a funny thing when you perform process improvement projects. You get down and dirty to find out what is really going on as you document the "as-is" process.

As you do this, you may stumble upon some very unexpected steps in the process—some of which may be illegal.

What do I mean by illegal? I am not talking about uncovering illegal kickbacks or anything that severe. What I am describing, however, is uncovering steps that are procedurally illegal due to some law, statute, or regulation.

This is more common in public sector organizations in which many of their processes are dictated by Congress or by an Executive Order. However this is also common with private companies that are heavily regulated, such as utilities; banks; defense contractors; and insurance companies.

Many of their processes are sprinkled with requirements dictated by law. When you uncover one of these "minor deviations" and present it to management in a weekly project briefing, you may end up spending more time with their general counsel than you had planned to.

Don't assume that this can't possibly happen to you, because it really does happen.

Union Resistance

Remember that altering processes is emotional and will likely alter employee job responsibilities. For these reasons, any organization that is represented by formal unions will pose yet one more obstacle with which to contend.

It often takes a significant amount of time to gain union approval for process changes. Therefore, if you have to deal with a union shop, plan on spending a lot of time with them. Obviously, you should work with them from the beginning in the attempt to gain their confidence and achieve at least some level of implicit approval.

Customer Focus

Focusing on the customer is key. Many people get wrapped up in process modeling the internal processes, focusing on these as the key issue for improvement and not focusing on the customer.

We all have customers, either internal to the organization or external. Each process has an outcome that serves some customer or some other form of a stakeholder.

When starting each process model, pay extra attention to the outcome. What is the outcome; when does it occur; what do the customers of that process get now; what would they like to get?

What would they like to get? That brings up a good point. Interview the customer of each process. Do not rely on the employees and management of that process; talk to the customers. You might be surprised at what they have to say.

知

Who is the best person to perform process improvement tasks? Definitely someone with good people skills. Personally, I like to use non-IT staff to carry out these tasks. Former IT sales people, in my experience, have worked best. They have at least a general IT knowledge, an understanding of user requirements, and the people skills that are critical for success. Whomever you select must be both good listeners and good politicians.

I also strongly suggest you use an automated tool, such as Visio, to assist in the process model documentation. This allows you to quickly change a process, save it as a different version, and print it out for use with the staff for whom you are working.

If you expect a lot of disagreement on each specific process, you may want to try a fully automated "electronic meeting" or "electronic facilitation tool" to discuss the processes or other requirements.

In electronic facilitation, each staff member in the meeting has a PC connected to a server. The specialized software will give each person the opportunity to type in his or her opinions and comments in a structured manner without knowing who is really saying what. This is great for letting employees express their true concerns and suggestions in a logical manner without having to worry about management or their colleagues knowing what they said.

You should also consider bringing both employees and management into the process improvement effort. When people are part of the team, they are more likely to feel as though their ideas will amount to something and that they are part of the solution. There is also a much better chance of accepting the outcome. Obviously you cannot do this with every employee who may be affected, so you must work to select this group wisely.

You should also capture metrics associated with each process or each sub-process. Capture such benchmarks and measurements as: how long it takes to accomplish the process; how often the result is used as an input into another task; the number of employees the task/sub-task currently affects; exception handling rates; etc.

These metrics will give you an excellent understanding of the current process and the improved process, and they will be critical to the ROI analysis.

知

In summary, be prepared to conduct some form of process improvement and decide to what extent you are willing to go. Obtain management's approval at all steps, and keep them informed on a regular basis. Expect resistance from everyone, and plan for it in both your project schedule and in a mitigation plan.

Determine how you will deal with the *process landmines,* such as:

- Conflicting Information
- Approved Process Deviation
- Only Listen to Me
- The Power Grab
- Illegal Activities
- Union Resistance (if applicable)
- Lack of Customer Focus

Let management know up front that there will likely be issues that will need their input for resolution, and be realistic concerning how long such a process improvement effort will likely take. If you don't know, take a guess, and then double it. That may sound unprofessional, but my experience has taught that it is very hard to judge the extent of such an effort. I have led process improvement tasks that should have taken six months, but end up never finishing, even after two years. In such a case, it is usually due to a lack of managerial support or their inability to make decisions.

There are many excellent books relating to process improvement. You should familiarize yourself with several. Be forewarned, however, that they are often based upon a specific methodology and use specific process modeling methods, so you must determine which method will work best in your situation.

Section Three

Implementing Successful Solutions

"Make everything as simple as possible, but not simpler."

— *Albert Einstein (1879-1955)*

Chapter Thirteen

Enterprise Portal Solutions

Traditionally, content repositories are accessed from their own applications, each with its unique user interface. These "stovepipe" applications allow us to query structured data via various database applications, while unstructured data is accessed through either a "text search and retrieval" application or through metadata searches. Content repositories include data on the Internet and corporate Intranet, which also comes with it is own unique search capabilities and web browser interface.

Most users today interact with and retrieve data from content sources distributed throughout the enterprise. Databases contain production data, and departments, such as Operations, may post their data via an Intranet application. Then there is the e-mail system, records management repositories, and customer relationship management (CRM) and enterprise resource planning (ERP) systems. The list of content sources can seem endless.

When I worked for a Fortune 500 company, I maintained a list of 38 key repositories that contained content that I often needed. There were many more than 38 repositories, but those were the ones that I relied on to perform my normal duties. These 38 repositories had a mix of interfaces and, worse yet, they all had individual user names and passwords. So I, like everyone else, simply wrote the user names and passwords down on a piece of paper. Being a high-tech professional, however, I also entered the user names and passwords into my personal information manager (PIM), which conveniently synchronized to my e-mail, Microsoft Outlook. All this sensitive data ended up being located in two electronic locations and one paper-based location. Multiply that by the 80,000 employees in the company and you can see why hackers have such an easy time accessing corporate resources.

There is a solution to all of this - one that comes the closest to offering Knowledge Nirvana. This solution is the *enterprise information portal*, or simply *"portal."*

A portal, often called the "killer app" of knowledge management, is a software application that allows the user to seamlessly access multiple content repositories from a single interface. It provides a single point of access to satisfy your content needs. The three minimum requirements for an enterprise portal are:

- Provide a single interface at all times for the user.
- Search multiple content repositories that contain both structured and unstructured data.
- Allow the user to issue a single search query and receive a single hit list of results.

The key is to allow the user to operate from a single application, with a single interface, and issue a single query on multiple repositories.

Having such a tool can greatly decrease the confusion and complexity of needing to access multiple repositories, such as 38 of them in my case. As an added benefit, a portal can solve one of the Holy Grails of information security—that of providing a single security sign-on for user names and passwords.

Note that accessing different data types is one of the key requirements for a portal. The reasons for this are twofold. First, as has been described previously, enterprise content resides in multiple formats, from Word documents; to e-mail; to structured databases. Therefore to add any real value to the user, a portal must be able to access different content containers simultaneously.

The second reason for this requirement is to distinguish a portal from all the product vendors who call their query application a portal. Let's say you developed a database application that allows the user to issue a query against two databases, which is not a hard feat for any humble programmer. That simple application would meet the requirement of accessing multiple repositories (two in this case). So do not be fooled by the many software product vendors that call their product a portal just because it provides a user interface and allows the user to query a repository or two.

Let's return to the security issue of maintaining user names and passwords. If a portal is going to allow you to access multiple repositories, then it should also manage your user account information of user names and passwords. With a true portal, the user should be able to log in only once, and that one time would be a login to the portal itself. The portal would then take care of the user account information for each relevant content repository.

If I issued a query from my portal on, let's say, a Cisco error message that I am getting during my futile effort to reprogram a router, the portal would distribute my query to a number of content repositories. The resulting hit list would then be displayed as one combined results list. These results would likely be categorized in some personalized manner, such as content relevancy and its location. The content container, or repository, may also be shown; e.g., the content resides in a Word document or a PDF file. All of this should be fully customized and personalized per individual user.

The enterprise portal may sound a lot like any of the consumer portals that we all use to search the web, such as Yahoo or Lycos; and you are right. Both types of portals are in some ways similar. The consumer portals allow the user to search multiple repositories and even add some degree of personalization. However the enterprise portal that provides the modern enterprise with a significant new capability is much more that a consumer portal. The enterprise portal:

- Supports many content types, not just HTML.
- Works inside the firewall, accessing both structured and unstructured repositories as well as CRM and ERP systems.
- Is highly customizable, allowing the user to personalize the interface and all aspects of the query and results list.

- Manages security user names and passwords through a single sign on.

An enterprise portal may also add push content delivery, as well as the more traditional pull delivery. Push and pull refers to the way in which content is provided to the user. In a standard query, one pulls the content from a repository. This requires active participation by the user; i.e., he or she has to request it. Push, on the other hand, is passive. The portal, or any other such application, pushes content to the user without the user specifically requesting it. An example of push content is general news about the organization, such as the latest press release or stock quote.

Portals are often much more than simply a single interface into multiple repositories. Adding additional functionality, such as collaboration and groupware capability, will also provide more value to the user. Collaboration functionality may include white-board capability, instant chats, and threaded discussions, all of which can be added to a highly customizable portal. Furthermore, a portal may become the interface for line of business applications or, at the very least, be highly integrated into those applications.

If successful, one should find that users spend most if not all of their time working from the portal, rarely needing to exit the portal to access other applications directly.

Expanding the user-base of a portal to include the organization's supply-chain partners is another common use of the enterprise portal. It is not uncommon to provide a limited functionality portal to those trading partners, so that they, too, have a single interface into your organization to access all the relevant data they are authorized to access. This may include production data for your product transport carriers, such as long-haul truck shippers or purchasing agents from your major customers. An accounts payable portal would allow a major supplier the ability to submit invoices and review their status.

The portal may also become the standard presentation interface for application-specific systems, such as data entry for your ERP system or for e-learning.

Yet another benefit of the portal is its ability to empower the virtual enterprise. As we increase our reliance on disparate teams working from numerous geographically distant locations, the portal provides access to the assets necessary to perform one's job regardless of location. This includes allowing everyone to access content as well as the other functionality, such as groupware and collaboration tools that are useful for geographically dispersed teams.

With the customization and personalization capability offered by an advanced enterprise portal, along with sophisticated security features, there are few limitations as we expand the functionality of the portal throughout the enterprise.

知

One area that may raise concern for an enterprise portal is the preservation of sensitive content when viewed through a portal.

Say your multinational Fortune 500 firm is planning to divest itself of its Latin American operations. This information is not yet public, but is known by most employees in the corporate headquarters and others in leadership positions. It is not a very sensitive corporate secret, obviously, but nevertheless, it is not yet releasable to the public.

Information concerning the divestiture is confidential and should be electronically marked in some manner to alert the reader of this confidentiality.

The resulting hit list from the portal's query usually includes a brief description of the content, such as its source; content type; and relevancy to the query. The format and type of results list is often highly customizable and may even allow the user to view an automatically generated summary of the content or the first three lines of the content. It may even extract the text out of the subject line in more structured content, such as e-mail.

In any case, the content is displayed in the portal's window and not through the native application.

Now let's say that you are preparing a briefing for some visiting securities analysts. Working in a dynamic organization, you are aware that content changes rapidly, so you use your enterprise portal to access the most updated company information, such as financial summary data; a list of company executives; and the organizational chart.

The results of your query include several corporate organizational charts. You want the more current one, so you naturally look for the one with the most recent date stamp. The most recent one should, in fact, contain the label "Confidential: Not For Release," but it may not be visible through the portal; i.e., the classification metadata may not necessarily be displayed through the portal.

You can imagine some of the problems that would likely arise at this point. Let's hope that the new version of the organizational chart isn't the one that lists the upcoming divestiture, otherwise you will be the one who prematurely releases that information.

Any organization that relies on a high volume, high velocity, and wide variety of sensitive data will have this metadata classification issue. The more one relies on data integration from different information containers, or performs data fusion, the more of an issue there will be of ensuring security metadata.

知

The ability to access disparate enterprise content is important, but not having it organized in a useful manner only compounds the "infoglut" challenge. Having content is fine, but not understanding its context makes that content much less valuable. It is therefore necessary to both prioritize the content and be able to efficiently navigate throughout the content.

For this reason, the portal must provide a common *taxonomy*. A taxonomy is an organized hierarchy of subjects that assist the user in both analyzing and navigating throughout the content.

Along with a customized taxonomy, other key evaluation criteria for an enterprise portal product include:

- Personalization—Can each user personalize the interface and other attributes? To what level of granularity is the product customizable?
- Security—Understand the security architecture of the portal product. What application controls security permissions, and where are user names and passwords stored? What is encrypted where? Can one define individual repositories to encrypt data upon transmission to the portal?
- Scalability—What is the ideal number of users of the portal: 50, 500, 5,000 per server? How do multiple servers interact?
- Comprehensiveness—What are the restrictions on the content repositories that can be accessed? Can the portal accept all forms of content; e.g., unstructured or voice and video?
- Integration—What tools are available for integration? What repository interfaces come pre-defined; e.g., Oracle, Microsoft Exchange, and Lotus Notes?
- Categorization—What automatic and customizable categorization of hit list results is provided? What are these formats?
- Taxonomy—What hierarchy and categorization options are provided? Is an automatic taxonomy creation option available?
- Presentation—How can the presentation be customized, per user, per repository?
- Searching—What search engine is natively supported by the portal? Can one substitute more advanced search engines?

知

While a small organization, say fewer than 300 users, may view a portal as simply an Intranet, a larger organization will require significant integration and customization of a portal product in order for it to be useful. Implementing such a portal is not trivial. For the portal to be useful, it must be highly integrated into both your content repositories and business processes. In many ways, implementing a portal involves the same complex integration issues that one faces with other mission-critical, enterprise-wide systems. Security needs must be met, legacy interfaces must be developed, availability must be ensured, and training and support will be required.

What makes portals even more difficult, however, is the need to access, interpret, and exchange data with a large number of content repositories. This is similar to the challenges faced with decision support systems, which have relied on complex data extraction tools. Portal product vendors have recognized this sometimes-limiting issue and usually offer pre-defined interfaces for many standard applications. Using these pre-defined interfaces should help in accessing standard applications, such as the newest version of e-mail repositories or other typical office documents. While these pre-defined interfaces do help, they do not alleviate the challenge of integrating the portal into the many existing, and often highly customized, applications currently in use throughout the enterprise.

As you can tell from this chapter, the enterprise portal offers a significant new productivity-enhancing tool for the knowledge worker. It can insolate the employee from those 38 separate repositories by focusing on a single application that can be highly personalized for each user's unique requirements, duties, and individual font size and color preferences.

For a portal to be useful, however, it must be highly customized, and that takes time and effort. A portal requires significant integration with each and every content repository that must be accessed. Having a portal that accesses only a few repositories would certainly be easier to deploy, but would only add meager value-added functionality. In my case, having 38 repositories and interfaces customized and offered in a single portal was well worth the investment in terms of my productivity, day after day, year after year.

When portals first came out as a "killer app," one product vendor offered a "portal in a box." While that vendor was certainly happy to sell such an out-of-the-box portal, such products cannot be seriously utilized in the modern enterprise. Advanced customization, personalization, and integration functionality is paramount for a portal to offer a high return on one's investment.

Because of the importance of the native software portal product, which forms the foundation of the customized portal application, the issue of product scalability becomes critical. The portal product must be architected in an open, flexible, and enterprise-strength manner. This will determine the scalability, extensibility, and future adaptability of your solution. Key issues to consider include:

- Operating system and database support
- Caching technology
- Load balancing
- Fail over capability
- Optimization and performance tuning tools
- User and repository management
- Performance with large number of concurrent users
- Synchronization with multiple portal servers

The difference between providing your organization with a significant productivity enhancement tool, rather than yet another "disruptive technology," will depend on a careful selection of the portal product, the level of integration, and a successful project implementation. The technology is available. How you implement that technology is what will make the difference.

"All wish to possess knowledge, but few, comparatively speaking, are willing to pay the price."

– Juvenal (60-140)
Roman satirical poet

Chapter Fourteen

Feeding the Portal

Paying the price for knowledge is what feeding the portal is all about. Juvenal was describing the years of reading, studying, and learning that were necessary for a Roman to gain knowledge. While still very true today on a personal level, the organization must also pay the price in its quest to effectively manage content.

In the previous chapter, you learned the value of the enterprise portal, which provides the single view into many disparate repositories and will likely become the predominant interface for a knowledge worker's applications.

There are, obviously, implementation and integration costs involved, but an equally significant cost comes from maintaining the portal's content repositories. That is the subject of this chapter.

知

There are two ways in which a portal can access content repositories. The first, and least desired way, is to have one repository into which all content is imported. Often called a "knowledge base," this single repository approach solves certain initial issues of integration by forcing the user to deposit, or register, their content with this new repository. This alleviates most of the need for the often-extensive integration efforts associated with multiple repositories.

The downside to all this, however, is substantial. Imagine that your organization is planning to implement a portal. Hurray! Then comes the e-mail announcement from IT that directs everyone, including you, to deposit your key content into this new repository.

What does that mean for you? More work.

There you are, already struggling under your normal workload, looking forward to the new tool announced by management, and then it hits you that this will require you to do more, not less.

Let's say that you are the financial administrator for the department. One of your standard functions is to run a weekly report and e-mail it to a set distribution list.

Now, with this new portal from management, you have yet another process appended onto your original weekly report process. You now have to copy the Excel spreadsheet file from your local disk drive to some server and register it with the portal. The registration requires you to fill out several metadata fields. All in all, not a hard thing to do, but it is more work.

Now multiply the added process of the financial administrator by hundreds or thousands of other employees, year after year, and that equates to a massive number of labor hours required to maintain the portal's content.

At this point, one of two things will likely happen.

Scenario one: the department's workload increases for whatever reason; e.g., an end-of-year sales increase, layoffs of some employees to help the bottom line numbers that quarter, or a higher than average turnover rate as employees jump to a new startup. Whatever the reason, people in the department start doing the unthinkable. They stop performing that added step of copying and registering their content to the portal.

If anyone notices this, it will probably be brushed off as just a temporary lapse; everything will get back to normal soon enough, and the portal will be refreshed with current content in no time.

Scenario two: the second way in which a centralized portal repository dies a sudden death is when the chief sponsor, cheerleader, and mentor of the portal project leaves. If the benefits and perceived value of the portal are not truly felt by most employees—

from senior management, to operations staff, to the administrative assistant—the departure of the key sponsor will kill the portal.

One IT company I worked for had a number of repositories and portals. In fact, it had lots of them; all dinosaurs. It started out with Lotus Notes, which provided many useful repositories and a portal-like application. It was a great tool for us, and served us well. Then the Intranet came along and every department and project had to have it's own web site, complete with animated gifs. People started adding content to their personalized Intranet pages, all but forgetting the repositories in Lotus Notes. Then we ended up switching to Microsoft Outlook, and people started adding content to the folders of Outlook. Next, self-service applications via an Intranet were in vogue, and we all but forgot Outlook folders.

Finally, we implemented a real portal: a commercial portal-in-a-box. This was not a real integration job, just an installation on a server. People started adding content to that portal, and those who used it loved it, for a while. Meanwhile we still had all those Intranet sites and Outlook, all full of outdated content.

What eventually killed the portal was license costs. The software cost per server, or per user, tends to be fairly steep. Steep enough that an organization must truly be committed to using a portal in order to justify the cost.

That brings up yet another issue concerning portals. For them to be useful there has to be both a sizable content base and a sizable user base. For this to occur, the portal must become ubiquitous throughout the organization. Otherwise, it will lack timely and accurate content needed to justify the cost of the portal, and the portal will be yet another failed IT project and a mere memory to the users.

The second way in which a portal can access timely and accurate content is through the integrated repository approach.

With the integrated repository, the user does not have to copy and register their content. The user simply performs their job functions, usually without any additional actions required on their part. With this approach, the various content repositories already in use throughout the organization are integrated with the portal. Your operation's Intranet site can be registered with the portal, as can your document or records management system. Structured databases can also be added to the portal by this means, as can real-time content, such as news or financial feeds.

Note that integrating a repository with a portal involves identifying the content type to the portal and establishing common metadata standards. How and when each portal is to scour each repository and update itself with new or changed content must also be configured.

This requires a substantial up-front effort to integrate all these repositories into the portal, so that the user of the portal can benefit from the single view and single query into the organization's primary content repositories. This work is often not trivial, but in the long run, it offers significant advantages over the single repository portal approach.

知

The single repository "knowledge base" approach is, however, useful in some select situations. If the organization recognizes that a collection of important information has never been captured in an electronic format, one may establish a *knowledge capture project.*

The purpose of such a project is to capture and organize key content that usually resides only with a select group of employees. Capturing their knowledge, to the best that we can, is often a last minute and desperate approach conducted right before an employee leaves the organization. This usually occurs just prior to retirement, when an organization realizes they are about to lose a valuable asset—a key employee and their tacit knowledge.

In this effort, the employee is the domain expert, sometimes called the *subject matter expert (SME).* The SME is then interrogated by "knowledge engineers" that seek to capture information and organize it in a repository. This repository is then called the *"knowledge base."*

For the most part, creating centralized knowledge bases offers limited benefit to the organization, for they capture information and processes in an artificial manner, complete with half-truths and missing issues from the mouths of the SMEs. These SMEs often distort the truth, consciously or not, and somehow fail to tell the inquisitive knowledge engineer key facts that may not be the most accurate.

知

Now your portal is up and running, fully integrated into the organization's primary content repositories. The users are accessing valuable organizational content, and the portal provides the latest content from many repositories throughout the enterprise and from third-party news and financial services.

Now you must maintain it.

There is a cost to maintaining even the integrated portal, but it should not be any more costly than maintaining any other near real-time mission-critical IT application.

One key difference is the physiological factor. Since a portal allows employees to access content in an easier and more efficient manner, the employees usually have an alternative source for the same content. Maintaining the users' trust that the portal is the preferred access mechanism for organizational content is paramount. If this trust starts to wither, users will revert back to calling their colleagues for that updated weekly financial report or will use e-mail to solicit ideas or seek content.

Maintaining this trust is more difficult than building the trust initially. Employees want access to data and information quickly to perform their jobs, and they will use the portal if they believe it will provide them with that content. Otherwise, they will use whatever other means are available, regardless of what management may direct them to do.

With that in mind, listed below are several maintenance issues that one should consider for the enterprise portal.

- Establish rules for content. Just like one should do for records management, define what documents are worthy of retention. Integrate records management personnel into this task; help them help you.

- Add more metadata. When most documents or other content are traditionally shared between communities of practice, they generally discuss, via e-mail or the telephone, what one is looking for and what can be provided. Therefore prior to the content being accessed, there is already some form of information sharing about the context; i.e., what it is, what it applies to, etc. With a portal or any other robust repository, the content may need more metadata than one currently uses. This metadata will be required to put the content into context for someone who is just now finding the content and is not a member of the content author's community of practice.
- System administration will be required. Like any other mission-critical system, the portal will require constant monitoring, tweaking, and other database-related administrative tasks.
- The single sign-on offered by a well integrated portal is powerful, but it requires constant maintenance. Passwords expire, users want access to new repositories, and employees come and go; all of which can put a real burden on the system administrator.
- Taxonomies change over time. Times change, vocabulary changes, and so do the organization's mission. All this change requires the taxonomy to be maintained in an orderly fashion. Establish a taxonomy committee to approve suggested changes to the baseline taxonomy.
- Finally, manage your bandwidth. If portals start providing your employees with new services and access to new content that they never had before, expect network bandwidth to spike sharply. Just imagine what happens to your bandwidth requirements when a junior employee wants to access a document collection consisting of the past twenty annual reports. Multiply that by hundreds or thousands, and you may find your telecommunications group cursing your project. Conduct a bandwidth analysis to determine the expected resources needed once portal usage takes off.

Work with your telecommunications group up front on this task.

知

The enterprise portal can indeed be the "killer app" for an enterprise, but feeding it—maintaining it—is a task that is just as important as the initial portal implementation and will require resources for proper management.

Keep in mind that a portal utilizes content repositories and other business applications but does not replace them. Those repositories also need managed with careful user administration and attention to data quality. All this content is then accessible through the portal, along with the added benefits of the portal application itself, such as groupware functionality and the single login.

"Accurate knowledge is the basis of correct opinions; the want of it makes the opinions of most people of little value."

– Charles Simmons (1798-1856)
American clergyman

Chapter Fifteen

Web Content Management

In an ideal world, the records management system, the enterprise's workflow solution, and the portal would all be integrated with every key repository and would effectively manage all content throughout the enterprise, without exception.

We have, however, always faced the challenge of developing an IT application that is both broad enough for general use and meets the unique functional requirements that justified the need for the new application in the first place. While every enterprise should be utilizing their records management system, which will effectively manage much of the organization's information, there remains some content that offers unique challenges. One of those unique challenges is web content management.

Most of our content today is written and formatted by the end-user, also known as the *"content creator."* It is developed for internal use with the content creator usually having a good idea who will read that document and what community of practice will act upon it.

Web content management is somewhat unique, since the content creator is usually neither the one formatting the content nor the one who has control over who will read and act upon it. Content on the Internet is also visible to the world and, therefore, the organization usually wants to ensure that it is a full and true representation of the organization's position, mission, and opinion. In cyberspace, web content represents the organization, just as an annual report represents the organization to others. For this reason, it is imperative that the content is correct in every manner; e.g., form, text, graphic appeal, and legal accuracy. This requires a formal review and approval process that can be managed by workflow.

Furthermore, a growing percentage of an organization's web content displayed to the world is dynamically generated. This content is transactional in nature and originates from back-end systems. For this, and the other reasons listed above, there exists software products that offer efficient and effective web site creation and content management. Many of the same principals of versioning, workflow, metadata, and classification apply to web content management, as it does to other managed content.

知

The publishing metaphor is appropriate for web content. Traditionally, one or more authors collaborate on the book or article; editors review and modify the content; then it is typeset, reviewed, and published. Throughout the publishing process, everyone knows what the process is and what he or she can and cannot do. The typesetter knows that he is not allowed to change text, and a final reviewer knows what his duties are. For the most part, this is an organized and controlled event, with a clear understanding of the content ownership at all steps throughout the process.

Creating and displaying web content is very much the same. One or more content creators (authors) collaborate on the content, at which time it may go to a manager or other reviewer for approval. With a web content management system, however, the approval process, as well as the entire content publishing process, can be routed and managed by workflow. Version control greatly supports this process by managing the content's version as it goes through the creation phase.

Because a web site usually contains a large quantity of content, multiple authors are typically involved. Early on, with the first generation of web content management systems, the issue of a consistent style and overall look-and-feel had to be addressed. The traditional "web master," often working with a graphic artist, creates templates for the content to ensure a standardized look-and-feel throughout the site. These templates also alleviate the authors from having to worry about such things as formatting, graphics, color scheme, and fonts. Templates also are key to supporting dynamic content on the site. The template can be populated by relatively static content from the traditional authors, and it can be populated by dynamic content taken from structured databases or even semi-structured document repositories.

Separating the authors from the format with a template is, most of the time, valuable. If you are creating a simple description of a new service or creating a press release, you may be willing to give up control of the format. Many times, however, authors have personal pride in their content and want to see how it will eventually look to the reader. Therefore it is important that your web content management system be flexible and offer the authors a means to view their content in the end format. This "what you see is what you get" (WYSIWYG) editing capability is something that many authors will want to utilize. Along with WYSIWYG, support of native authoring tools, such as Microsoft Word, is also available from most web content management products.

Separating the content from the format also has several other benefits. First, it alleviates what used to be the significant bottleneck in web site content—that of the web master. Early web sites, as well as many today that do not use a web content management system, still rely on one or two employees to control the web site—the Web Master(s). Having many content creators all feeding one or two Web Masters can quickly create a serious backlog of content.

A second benefit of separating content from format is the ability to quickly reformat the web site with minimal effort. No longer do you have to modify every page; e.g., to change a logo design. Now, only the templates need modified. This can save hundreds or thousands of labor hours when your organization eventually decides to redesign its web site.

Separating content from format, and separating both of these from business-logic in the case of transactional applications, requires managing finer-grained data elements. The traditional records management system manages whole containers of data or information, while web content is usually a finer-grained level of content. This could include a standard logo graphic file, standardized text for the footer of the web page, and the primary content coming from several sources of both unstructured text and near real-time dynamic structured text.

Managing dynamic content also increasingly involves using the eXtensible Markup Language (XML). XML-tagged documents allow the user to easily share content within the document, thus providing an ability to easily customize and personalize the document. This ability is not available with traditional HTML-based web documents.

Again, there exist specific web content management products that are optimized to use XML content. These products, therefore, will likely be needed as an enterprise increases its use of XML-based documents.

知

Dynamic web site creation is quickly becoming a common requirement, since we expect a web site to be an accurate source for near real-time content personalized for the reader. It must combine both static and dynamic content, the latter of which usually comes from a backend data repository. It aggregates content from multiple repositories and personalizes it for the reader.

Accessing a supplier's web site catalog, for example, may render a different view and different content to the reader based on any of a number of personal factors, such as the location of the Internet Protocol (IP) address or from "cookies" that reside on the user's computer.

The dynamic web site must also take into consideration the format of the reader's display. Is the reader accessing the web site via a desktop computer, or is she accessing it from a hand-held mobile device or from a kiosk? For properly viewing the web site, and hence the content, the browser template should be substituted with a template for the appropriate display.

知

As should be obvious from this chapter, web site content management is very similar, yet different, from the more traditional data and information content management. It is similar in the need to efficiency route the content through a process via a workflow application. The authors of the web content benefit from the version control functionality and the collaboration capability offered to them.

The desire to integrate dynamic content and the need to optimize the interface, communications mechanisms, and support security all require specific protocols and server applications designed specifically for Internet and Intranet web services.

So what do you do?

Ideally you should utilize the same content and collaboration tools that are used throughout the organization. These records management systems, workflow tools, and portals (hopefully currently in use) provide the key enabling technologies for effective content management and team collaboration. Then why not use it for web content as well? You should, if you can. This will be based on the maturity of the software products you choose to implement, and the extent of XML and dynamic content from back-office systems that need incorporating into dynamically rendered web pages.

As is always the guidance, you should define your requirements, study the products currently available, and decide what combination of products will best meet your needs. The resulting "solution-set" will then require the integration and middleware to make the system truly useful for the enterprise.

"In theory, there is no difference between theory and practice. But, in practice, there is."

— Jan L. A. van de Snepscheut
Computer Scientist
California Institute of Technology

Chapter Sixteen

Successful Project Planning

Forget all those Dilbert jokes on project management. Managing any IT project is difficult, and managing a content or collaboration project can be especially tricky. There is so much that can go wrong, even without having technical problems. Hardware orders get delayed, key stakeholder meetings get canceled, your accounting department loses invoices, and staff members get stuck in snowstorms. The list is endless. Therefore a good IT project manager, one with real experience with both large programs and small tasks, from pure software development projects to systems integration jobs, is a valuable team asset.

I recently had the pleasure to hear Donald Trump speak - the man who made his mark on New York City, only to face bankruptcy by 1990 with the inability to make $2 billion of loan payments. "The Donald," as he is often referred to, rebounded as a result of his goal oriented focus and his remarkable ability to find and exploit a market niche. He talked about his successes and failures in business and offered his top ten list for success. Having never heard him speak, I was not sure what to expect. He was a most interesting speaker and I found his top ten list for success applicable to project management. So here is The Donald's top ten list for success, along with my own project management commentary:

1. Think big—It is fine to start with a pilot or a prototype implementation as a proof of concept, but other than that, think big. Content management, team collaboration, and process improvement offers the chance to make significant improvements to the enterprise. Think big and express that to management, your team, and all stakeholders.

2. Stay focused—Focus on success and all the details that must come together to achieve that success. As the project manager, you are the only one who is solely focused on the project in its entirety. Management is counting on you, as are your programmers, business analysts, and system architects. Stay focused.

3. Be paranoid—Assume that most everything is at risk. Regarding your staff, management, and stakeholders, the optimist would say you should trust but verify. The pessimist, who is probably the experienced project manager, would likely trust no one, and would validate or otherwise ensure that everything gets done properly. Did that code really pass acceptance testing? Did that purchase order really get sent out on time? Are the budget numbers accurate? Check and re-check everything and assume nothing before validating it (actually, Trump's "be paranoid" went on to say something to the effect that "everyone really is out to get you").

4. Keep your momentum going—It is easy to lose momentum on any IT project. As project manager, you are the coach, cheerleader, and motivational speaker that your staff will look to for guidance. It is easier to keep the momentum going than to regain it once lost. Keep all staff members and management informed through a project schedule so they can see for themselves the progress and the importance of meeting milestones.

5. Be passionate—If you don't believe in your project, no one else will. You must be passionate and articulate it. If there is any quiver in your voice as you describe the importance of your project, you have failed.

6. Go against the tide—Success may mean going against conventional wisdom, especially if conventional wisdom has led to stalemate or failure in the past. To strive for real change—real productivity change—you must take risks. You will anger some people and annoy others. Going against the tide will be necessary. Recognize that and be prepared.

7. Hire the best/work with the best people—Mediocre staff will likely lead to mediocre results. You need good people—people who can work in both a team and individually and who can think "out of the box." People can have their individual expertise and specialties, but a general baseline of experience in related fields is important. A programmer who has spent time doing requirements definition with actual users will have a better understanding of both business analysis and end-user expectations.

8. Be lucky—Yes, luck can be part of the equation. Sometimes everything falls into place like a well-oiled machine. Be thankful for it, but don't plan on it (see Be Paranoid).

9. Have some degree of certainty in your life—There are two ways in which this is applicable to project management. The first is that you have to trust some people some of the time. Have a degree of certainty that some people will support you and give you the benefit of the doubt. This is necessary to keep your sanity and to keep you coming to work every morning. Secondly, have a contingency plan in case your project goes south in a hurry. After all, you may not be lucky; budgets may suddenly shrink, your stakeholders may change, or your firm may be acquired, thus making your project overcome by events.

10. Get even—Self-explanatory coming from The Donald.

The remainder of this chapter discusses the key issues of managing a project, with a focus on content and collaboration projects. Risk, risk mitigation, staffing, and metrics are all addressed. The use of systems integrators, consultants, and software product vendors are also discussed, along with the four key issues to avoid.

Related to managing a project is how to execute the project, and is covered in the next chapter on methodologies. It covers the key aspects of project methodologies and processes necessary for content and collaboration projects.

As previously discussed, there is a great deal involved in successful project management - from financing to technical architecture to human resources. This chapter cannot teach you project management. Instead, it focuses on the key issues necessary for content and collaboration project management. Seven areas are briefly covered in this section, prior to discussing the four areas to avoid. The seven are: best management practices; metrics; risk and risk mitigation; staffing; tools; full disclosure; and integrators, consultants, and product vendors.

Best Management Practices

One of the key benefits of collaboration is the reuse of information and work products, so why should project management be any different?

There already exists a wide variety of documented best practices with which you can and should leverage for your project. Some of these are from trade associations, such as the American Management Association, or from industry-specific associations. Contact these associations to see what's available for use in project management and for other aspects of your project. This may include technical specifications, recommended workflows, and testing processes.

Another good source is the Software Engineering Institute (SEI) run by Carnegie Mellon University. They have established a formal approach to rating capabilities of organizations based on the seven levels of the Capability Maturity Model (CMM). Organizations on the higher levels of this model are required to have defined processes for most every aspect of the project, from software development to testing, metrics, and risk management. These processes, along with reusable assets such as templates and documentation, are available in process asset libraries. A resource called a *jump-start kit* includes all the documentation, guidance, and lessons learned needed to jump-start a new effort, such as establishing metrics or starting a quality assurance program. If you want to formalize your project, or at least look like you really know what you are doing, look to see what Carnegie Mellon has to offer.

Metrics

How will you know if your project succeeds? How about simply guessing or assume success based on the lack of complaints? I have seen my share of projects that measured success by the lack of complaints received at the help desk. What developers often fail to realize is that people may simply ignore the new system and, therefore, won't need to complain about it.

Metrics means the art of measurement. You need defined and tangible metrics to assess your project. The metrics can be used both during a project and upon completion to assess the level of success or failure. Metrics used during the project execution are usually easier to develop and track. These would include the number of milestones completed to date, the number of software modules completed, etc. Basically, this is simple project management.

Metrics that are used to ascertain the success or failure of the overall project can be harder to identify and adequately assess. This tends to get political and puts people squarely on the spot. Start with the project's objectives. Why was the project initiated in the first place? What are we trying to improve? If you can identify what you are trying to improve, quantify it; e.g., how many widgets will be improved by what degree?

There exist defined methodologies that can greatly assist in defining the objectives of a project based on metrics. One is the

Balanced Scorecard methodology. If you really want to formalize a project's objectives and metrics, use a well-established methodology such as the Balanced Scorecard.

Workflow metrics can be the easiest to measure, since you are improving the efficiency of defined work processes. Therefore if you are focusing on workflow, your job of establishing metrics will be relatively easy.

Related to metrics is the cost-benefit analysis. Most organizations use some form of cost-benefit analysis to determine if a project is worthy of funding. There are times, however, when such an analysis is not warranted. When you open a new office, do you perform a cost-benefit analysis to determine whether to install telephones? Of course not. Some projects are intuitive or otherwise don't need to undergo the riggers of a cost-benefit model.

Risk and Risk Mitigation

Risk is what management worries about on a new project. You need to think through what can go wrong (again, be paranoid; it helps in risk planning) and plan on how you will minimize that risk from cropping up once the project is underway.

Analyze all aspects of the project. Start by creating a generic list of key categories, or get them from other projects in your organization if such a list already exists. A typical list of categories may include:

- Expectations
- Schedule
- Staffing
- Financial
- Technical

Once you have these generic categories, assess your own project in relation to each category. What are the schedule slippage issues? What milestones may not be met? Ask yourself these and other questions, briefly documenting those that are likely to both happen and are serious enough to affect the project's overall success.

Next, you need to establish a risk mitigation plan for each risk identified. How would you mitigate the risk? What actions can you take now or in the near future?

Once you have the risks listed by category and the mitigation strategy for each risk, document them in the form of a matrix. Use that matrix for management and your staff so that everyone is aware of the risks. Don't hide the matrix or use it only for yourself. Periodically update the matrix, such as before each project review meeting, which should be scheduled regularly.

Staffing

Heed Donald Trump's advice and hire the best, whether they be employees, system integrators, or consultants (see *Integrators, Consultants, and Product Vendors*).

You will likely need a variety of technical and managerial disciplines on your team, from programmers to database administrators, business analysts, and process modelers. Worry first about what skills are needed, then determine how you will acquire those skills. To simply decide how you are going to utilize existing staff may be tempting, but it is too easy to overlook needed skills. Staff top-down, not bottom-up.

Tools

From a project management perspective, software tools and applications exist that can greatly assist both the project manager and the team.

Most of you are probably familiar with standard project management tracking tools such as Microsoft Project. It is a fairly robust and easy-to-use tool that everyone managing a project should utilize. It also scales well, serving all but the largest of projects.

There are also tools available that are designed to assist in process improvement efforts. These tools include everything from

process and data diagramming tools to complete enterprise repositories designed for process improvement and legacy system conversion.

It is highly recommended that you use one of these simple
diagramming tools to assist in creating your as-is and to-be models.
These tools are easy to use and will save countless hours in drawing
mundane boxes and arrows. These tools are usually optimized for
one or more of the standard modeling methodologies, such as IDEF,
so pick a tool that supports your modeling methodology.

On the high-end are enterprise-wide tools that include repositories designed for process improvement components, such as
process and data models. While these are nice, they are not necessary if you are already using a repository accessible by all team
members.

Full Disclosure

Communication, at all times, is vital to success. People must
know what is expected of them and how the project is proceeding.
Don't hold anything back; communicate. Bad news does not get
better with time.

The concept of full disclosure, for everyone on the project,
promotes communication flow. Being up front with your staff will
set a good example and will help them in their often natural reluctance to discuss serious issues.

Integrators, Consultants, and Product Vendors

You are probably not going to implement a solution exclusively
with in-house resources. Instead, like most projects today, you will
utilize others to augment your staff. These partners may come in the
form of full-service system integrators, specialized consultants, and
software product vendors.

You must decide how best to augment your staff with these partners, who often have an overlap in capabilities. Some organizations

basically outsource their entire project to a system integrator, assigning only a project manager who is less of a day-to-day project manager than a reviewer of deliverables and signer of invoices. This method can work well if an entire system is to be deployed and is well understood and documented. You are, however, relying on the systems integrator almost exclusively to succeed. The risk, therefore, can be high.

The selection of the systems integration team is much more critical than selecting the systems integrator. Let me explain and start with an example. I was a consultant to a $64 billion organization that wanted to implement a content management and workflow system for a key process in their national headquarters. The project was contracted to a major integration firm, whose name will not appear to protect the guilty. Their management pulled together a team of business analysts and programmers, which was led by a project manager. For some unknown, and what can only be described as crazy reason, this highly visible project was assigned a project manager who had never before implemented content management or workflow. Worse yet, the lead programmer was someone right out of college, who we later discovered did not even know how to use a variable in programming.

Yes, this was crazy and bizarre, but it happens in greater frequency than it should. Preventing this from happening is actually rather simple. For the most part, forget the company name and logo on the business card, and pay more attention to the individual staff assigned to the proposed project than the company for which they work. The company may have a great reputation, but that reputation will not contribute much to success. The experience and capabilities of each staff member is what counts. Insist on reviewing and approving each person, assessing his or her individual capabilities.

It is also possible to use systems integrators for just a phase of the project, such as the programming phase or for training and support. In general, however, most systems integration projects are full life cycle projects, from system architecture through deployment. This may or may not include the initial requirements definition phase or the training and support phases at the end of the life cycle. Systems integrators prefer to do it all and use their methodologies, tools, and personnel.

On the other hand, consultants dislike performing the entire project life cycle, preferring instead to focus on one or two phases of the project. Consultants can be valuable to a project, for they bring detailed tacit knowledge gained through years of hands-on experience.

The consultant can significantly alleviate risk by identifying issues early on and suggesting mitigating actions. Consultants are also good at criticizing, and therefore are excellent at reviewing the progress of systems integrators. In fact, there is an industry known as *independent verification and validation* (IV&V) that provides this form of contracted oversight to projects. Depending on the complexity and scope of the project, the use of an IV&V consultant may be warranted.

Consultants may also provide value by performing one or more limited phases of the project, the most common being the requirements definition phase. Requirements definition itself can be a tricky task to pull off successfully. There are some people who are experienced at it and others who are not. Defining the requirements, both functional and technical, will form the basis of the project and will be used by the integration or programming team to develop the system. Therefore, overlooking a key requirement may lead to significant budget overruns, as the project backtracks to compensate for that *newly discovered requirement*.

The third type of partner for your project is the software product vendor. You will certainly utilize them, for you will not want to build your own portal or workflow product. Instead, use commercially available products as the foundation of your solution.

Some products are general purpose in nature, and it is likely that you and your staff will have already used them on other projects. These general-purpose products include databases, programming languages, and configuration management tools. Our focus, however, needs to be on the newly utilized products, such as the content and collaboration products that your organization is considering.

One needs to perform due diligence on both the product itself and the product's vendor. You can leverage the expertise of niche consulting firms in product evaluation as well. For the products you are seriously considering, you should evaluate each by:

• Conducting an interview with current customers to learn the details about the product and how the product's vendor truly supports it.

• Examining each vendor's position in their market space and examining their finances (will they likely still be in business in 18 months?).

• Having vendors prove themselves with a pilot or prototype implementation before you commit to the enterprise.

• Clarifying the responsibilities of any interfaces that exist with other applications, and determining what operating systems, databases, and applications the vendor has actually tested.

• Not accepting boilerplate terms and conditions (T&Cs) of the sales contract. Add your own protective clauses.

The use of systems integrators, consultants, and software product vendors is a necessity to ensure a timely implementation. Knowing your acquisition and implementation strategy prior to starting the project will allow you to select the best mix of partners. There is good talent out there; use it.

知

While there are many things that can go wrong with a project, there are a few that occur more often than others. The top four issues that can derail a project the quickest are discussed below, along with what you can do to prevent them from happening.

Lack of Executive Sponsor Commitment

Implementation of a solution that will have the transforming effect required to attain a competitive advantage will be very difficult and will require the coordination of many people. These people will probably be from various departments within the organization. Each department will likely have competing objectives, diverse content repositories, different work processes and reporting standards.

To work through this will be a challenge - one that requires the cooperation of these people and their management. To get that cooperation, a senior executive of the organization must express commitment to the project.

Expressing commitment entails much more than sending an e-mail or making a speech at the project kick-off meeting. The executive sponsor must be truly be supportive, must believe in the project, and must continuously communicate that fact to all relevant parties. That sponsor will also be needed to facilitate issues that may arise and to negotiate resolutions. It is important that they recognize that some of their time will be necessary throughout the life of the project; hopefully not much, but they will need to attend certain meetings and approve various recommendations.

Poorly Defined Requirements

Poorly defined requirements represent the quickest way to achieve project death. Defining the requirements properly is critical. Not everyone is skilled and experienced to the point of performing a comprehensive requirements definition task successfully. The first thing you must do is ensure that you have the right skills necessary to perform such a task. Defining requirements accurately is an art, not a science, and requires good people skills. Having the mind of an investigator is important, since one will be ferreting out issues and will need to know what questions to ask when.

Both functional and technical requirements will need to be defined. Functional requirements are those like "the system shall display the widget status" or "the system shall allow input of the widget order form." Technical requirements, which tend to come from the technical staff more than the typical end-users, define which operating environment the system shall support. They also define what performance requirements must be met and how many users are to be supported.

Defining the requirements early is imperative. This requires gathering and analyzing the requirements from all stakeholders as early in the project as possible. It is also important to baseline the requirements and get consensus on those requirements from all stakeholders.

The issue of changing requirements once they have been established is challenging. Once baselined, should you agree to the changes? If the proposed changes do not significantly add value to the system, try putting them off. We all want to offer a system that exceeds expectations, but changing requirements in mid-stream has been known to kill its share of projects.

Naive Expectations

There are times when expectations exceed reality. This is not to say that great things are not possible, just that some stakeholders' expectations may require more of an effort to implement than they are worth; i.e., the benefit of the project is not adequate relative to the anticipated cost.

I was managing one project that found itself attempting to automate knowledge, which is impossible. My requirements definition team went out and worked extensively with the stakeholders, compiling a comprehensive requirements document. However, after I read it in its totality, it became obvious that the users were asking for a system that would automate their entire jobs, including their complex thought processes. If I could have built such a system, it would have replaced them all; not that they realized that. It is much easier to manage expectations up front rather than backpedal as you try to explain why something is not feasible.

Poor Communications

There is no excuse for poor communications. Communicating your objectives in a precise and articulate manner is part of a professional demeanor.

There are other communications problems, however, that can arise. Your stakeholders may not communicate all their requirements, constraints, or priorities. People also do not like to be the bearer bad news, so many people naturally ignore, or fail to bring up, key issues. We also have the issue of not speaking the same "language." IT people tend to speak differently than most business professionals, and vice versa.

What can you do? A lot, actually. Standard management reporting, based on your predefined metrics, offers a good and subjective way to communicate the project's status. The status, in relation to the risk mitigation plan, should offer good clues on how your project is progressing. Document everything, and get buy-in from the stakeholders by having them review documents and signing off on the requirements.

知

Everyone needs a methodology to implement a content or collaboration system. Your methodology may be rather ad hoc and based on your personal experience. That is acceptable to some degree, but it is neither professional nor effective in the long run.

The whole idea behind the Capability Maturity Model (CMM) is to define best practices and standards of various methodologies and processes. At level five (CMM Level 5), the processes are continuously optimized and refined. The purpose behind this is to evolve from a "hero mode" to a defined, repeatable, and optimized mode of operations (the hero mode refers to a project that operates based on the experiences and guidance of one or more heroes, as opposed to utilizing a proven repeatable process). If you operate in the hero mode, you may want to consider adopting a more structured methodology, processes, and work products.

A methodology consists of two primary entities: a strategy and processes. The work products, mentioned above, are outputs, such as reporting charts; project charts; staffing plans; and risk mitigation matrices. These can be optimized and repeatable assets.

The strategy is the overall approach, concept of operations, and macro-level plan. The processes define the detailed steps or techniques to achieve a specific objective. This may be a risk mitigation process that details how one should define the risks and the mitigating strategy.

Methodologies can be macro level or micro level. The Knowledge Nirvana methodology is a macro level methodology that guides one through content and collaboration systems deployment. Other methodologies define specific processes, such as data modeling. The IDEF methodology, discussed previously, is a methodology that provides a strategy and specific process for defining process and data models; i.e., it is fairly specific in its objectives. Therefore there is not one methodology that you should use. Rather, you need to select and then use various methodologies, some that cover the macro-level strategy and others detailed in their objectives and processes.

"The hallmark of engineering discipline is predictability: predictable cost, predictable schedule, predictable quality, and predictable functionality."

— Carnegie Mellon University's Software Engineering Institute

Chapter Seventeen

The Knowledge Nirvana Methodology

The Knowledge Nirvana methodology is designed to assist you and your organization on implementing successful content and collaboration solutions. Other methodologies certainly do exist, and you should use them if your organization has previously standardized on one or more of those methodologies and related practices and processes. In either case, the Knowledge Nirvana methodology outlined in this chapter will provide specific content and collaboration guidance that you should find useful regardless of what methodology you will ultimately use.

It is important that you use some form of methodology. As Yogi Berra stated, "If you don't know where you're going, you might not get there," and a structured methodology allows you to plan where you are going.

Please note that the name *Knowledge Nirvana*, while the name of this book, is also the name given to this methodology, and is both a servicemark and a (pending) registered trademark. While use of the name and the methodology outlined in this chapter may be used for your individual project implementations, please ensure that both ownership of the name and methodology and identified and that credit is given to the owner (example: Knowledge Nirvana[SM] Copyright 2002 by Jüris Kelley). Thank you.

知

The Knowledge Nirvana methodology consists of the five strategic phases that are designed to ensure a successful project implementation by both spending "quality time" at the beginning of the project and ensuring sufficient resources to "hand-hold" the end-users at the conclusion of the project. These are the two most often overlooked aspects of a project, and thus deserve added attention and detail in the project methodology.

There are five phases, including: *strategic planning*; *enterprise process improvement*; *architecture definition*; *integration and application modernization*; and *system implementation and operations*.

Keeping with the content reuse philosophy, each phase utilizes and feeds a content repository. A description of the content repository immediately follows the description of each of the five phases.

Strategic Planning

Understanding the true objectives, mission, and human and political factors associated with a proposed system is often overlooked by many people straining to meet project goals within budget. Unremitting political factors, social communities of practice, and other nuances often are overlooked and yet can contribute to a project's demise. Therefore one should take time up front to analyze these issues.

In this first phase, you must obtain a good understanding of the macro-level view of the organization, as well as an understanding of the significant issues, not just the most obvious ones. Also, identify all relevant stakeholders and previous projects that may have attempted to solve the same requirements.

The other four methodology phases each have a defined output, which becomes the input to the following phase. This *Strategic*

Planning phase, however, uses for its input the relevant mission, goals, plans, and objectives of the enterprise. Consider outside dependencies, such as funding and political support.

You will need to establish a solid understanding of the enterprise prior to proceeding. This is accomplished by performing tasks such as:

- Planing the plan.
- Analyzing mandates and reviewing the mission and employee values.
- Performing an external scan of all stakeholders and organizational dependencies.
- Performing an internal scan of resources, current strategy, existing performance expectations, and infrastructure standards.
- Identifying strategic issues facing the organization
- Developing the overall strategy and establish the acquisition strategy.
- Performing the culture audit and knowledge audit
- Establishing change management practices and acceptance reviews.
- Establishing integrated operational planning for the project.

The enterprise mission and values, for example, require one to establish performance goals, define quantifiable objective metrics, establish performance indicators, and relate the goals to the performance indicators. Use existing vertical methodologies as needed, such as the Balanced Scorecard methodology for the enterprise's performance metrics.

Strategy development includes an analysis of the future business models, performing a gap analysis and defining the strategies to fill these gaps.

Enterprise Process Improvement

The importance of improving existing processes has been discussed throughout this book. Due to this importance, and the fact that many projects fail to perform process improvement, it deserves its own high-level phase in the methodology.

Process improvement, or business process reengineering (BPR), includes the planning, analysis, design, and defining characteristics of process flows, functional models, and data elements.

As-is models are defined from process flows and business rules. Storing these as-is models in the reuse library will allow you to efficiently create the to-be models. The use of process simulation can then be used to help you optimize the various models.

Like the *Strategic Planning* phase, your process improvement efforts should utilize appropriate vertical methodologies, such as IDEF0.

Architecture Definition

Establishing the overall architecture is key prior to deciding upon the system design, approach, and products to be utilized to form the overall solution-set of the system. The architecture often includes:

- Functional domain models that feed the functional architecture requirements list.
- Evaluation of current and future technologies.
- Functional architecture requirements.
- Performance cost models.
- Information assurance requirements and cost models.

Developing an open systems architecture for the enterprise is vital for long-term operations and flexibility.

The current architecture environment should be documented and, with project concepts, will allow you to develop and subsequently analyze architectural what-if models. New technology evaluations are taken into account to create the target architecture.

An infrastructure modernization initiative should then be established, based on the technical architecture and the catalog of approved IT products for the organization.

Identifying the target organization's level of technical acceptance and risk is also important. Mapping the organization to one of the technology adoption models, which often range from *technology laggards* through *early adopters*, can be helpful.

Integration and Application Modernization

Most systems today will be modernized, as opposed to completely replaced. As we implement the enterprise portal, for example, it will be integrated with legacy systems and their repositories. Likewise, collaboration systems will likely need to import and feed existing legacy systems. Therefore the focus of this phase is integration and the modernization of existing systems.

Even if an existing system is replaced, there will always be some value, which can be extracted from the legacy system, whether it be business rules, code, procedures, or data. Referred to as *system re-engineering methodologies*, there exist best-practice methodologies for extracting useful value from an existing application or system.

Technical and functional requirements should be defined, along with a comprehensive test plan with acceptance criteria to ensure that both the integrators and developers understand the expectations. This should also serve as an objective set of testable requirements.

New software development can be performed using either a spiral or waterfall approach, depending on the detailed requirements and the organization's competence with either of these two general approaches to software development.

The application architecture, commercial off the shelf technologies, reuse libraries, data models, and project management libraries all feed the conversion, integration, and new software development efforts. An output of this phase should be the establishment of an application library that is comprised of the data models, functional models, and code available for reuse.

System Implementation and Operations

In an ideal world, the solution would be developed based on detailed and comprehensive requirements that resulted in a complete and uniform implementation with happy users and smiling stakeholders; but then there is reality.

Specific site plans need to be established to ensure basic issues, such as ensuring that there is ample electrical power. The planned system design will likely be molded with the current environment to create a composite systems model. Site specific configurations are then developed for implementation. Configuration management libraries are updated with site specific configurations and other site anomalies.

An operational system is achieved only after a comprehensive training plan is executed that includes extensive user feedback. This "hand-holding" of the individual users is a small price to pay in comparison to the overall program investment.

Technology refresh is an important operational consideration. You should define the refresh cycle times, such as every six months or eighteen months. This includes both updating system components, such as databases versions and patches, and taking into account new infrastructure updates, such as the new version of Microsoft Windows or the latest browser.

Operationally, we expect nothing less that 24x7 in today's society, so adequate support may become a serious issue if not identified early on as a requirement.

Content Repository

The central repository provides a managed and controlled environment for all project content assets. Project management assets generally fall into three categories:

- Process Asset Library—This repository, often called a "library" to distinguish its formal and approved content assets, should be the location for all non-management-related reusable content, such as modeling methodologies; implementation jump start kits; boilerplate wording; etc.

- Project Management Library—This repository provides a centralized resource for all project management-related assets, such as management reporting documents; human resource forms; etc.
- Project Repository—This provides a project-specific repository for all content assets, such as work plans; to-be models; and source code.

知

The use of a specific enterprise methodology is invaluable to ensure project success and system deployment in a risk-reduced manner. The use of specific vertical methodologies, practices, and procedures compliment the enterprise methodology. Therefore there is no one methodology, just as there is no one single solution for all. Instead it is a patchwork of methodologies, processes, and procedures that you must assemble based on your unique environment, resources, complexity, and organizational philosophy. You, as project manager, must select those patches on their own merit and organizational fit, weaving them together to form the project.

As I hope you recognize from this chapter and the preceding one on project management, a project can operate in either the "hero mode" or operate as a controlled, defined, and repeatable mode of operations that benefits from the collective experiences of others. Part of that collective experience is found in the reuse of content assets, which have been optimized and thus allow one to be more efficient.

Methodologies and processes are also vital to effectively managing a project. Use of a defined methodology will guide you and your staff through the project life cycle.

The Knowledge Nirvana methodology is shown in an abridged fashion in this chapter. This is not intended to be a comprehensive review of the methodology, but rather an overview that identifies key attributes of each phase.

So use what you have learned from the methodology, as well as the rest of this book, as you go forth and implement solutions that harness the untapped productivity of the enterprise and leverage the knowledge that exists within each employee.

"Victory goes to the player who makes the next-to-last mistake."

— *Savielly Grigorievitch Tartakower*
Chessmaster (1887-1956)

Chapter Eighteen

95 Knowledge Nuggets (Tips) for Success

Much has been covered in this book, and I truly hope that you will use what you have learned as you strive to accelerate your organization's cycle of innovation. With this in mind, I have highlighted some of the key lessons learned and recommendations that I have found to be invaluable throughout my own struggles with improving organizational productivity. Some of these tips—or *knowledge nuggets*—may seem obvious and simple in nature, but remember, it is usually the simple and obvious that sidetrack a project. So do not take them lightly.

Now, here is an exercise for you. Take out a pencil and read each tip. Make a notation in the margin next to each tip that you feel in any way may be an issue on your project. Also, make a similar notation for each tip that you simply had not thought of before. Don't dismiss any of them; make the notation and come back later to review each one.

As you perform this simple exercise, play the role of devil's advocate, or as Donald Trump would likely say, *be paranoid*. If the project does not have a firm handle on the subject of that tip, mark it down for later review. Be objective and be demanding on yourself and your project. You will be better off in the end if you do this.

So here they are: the *95 Knowledge Nuggets for Success*:

1. Don't treat Knowledge Management as a fad. KM is a discipline that combines people, processes, and technology that focuses on managing organizational content and individual knowledge as a corporate asset. The buzzword may fade away, but the power of a properly utilized system is invaluable.

2. Pass the "so what test." You may have management's commitment and support from some stakeholders, but in the end, the project will need to be perceived as adding value for all. So what value does it add, per stakeholder, user, and customer?

3. Formally justify the investment of such an important project. Once the macro-level business case objective has been determined, justify the initiative based on a real cost justification methodology. If your organization does not have such a return on investment (ROI) standard, try using the Balanced Scorecard methodology for IT justifications. This does not have to be an elaborate effort; just do it.

4. Have a commitment of funds. Management needs to know how much this will eventually cost. Sure it can be incrementally funded, but correlate funding to documented successes and relate this to the overall program plan and funding strategy. Understand this from the outset.

5. Spend a few dollars on promotional giveaways. A mouse pad or stuffed teddy bear with the project's name, logo, and tag line will go a long way to build team harmony and tangibly imply commitment to the project.

6. Define all stakeholders involved in the project. Stakeholders are all the people who have some interest or stake in the outcome of the initiative. This includes much more than just your typical end-users. Stakeholders can include senior management, finance, suppliers, vendors, etc. Spend some out-of-the-box time thinking this through.

7. E-mails are nice, but conduct real project review briefings. People like to see you in person. While keeping management and others in the loop with e-mails or other status

reports, do not overlook the value of face-to-face update briefings.

8. Identify and manage the luddites. Luddites are those who despise your project and will be a complainer at the very least and a saboteur at the worst. Determine who they are, why they are that way, and work them into your Risk Mitigation Plan.

9. Identify the gatekeepers of content reuse. Every organization has gatekeepers who manage actions and are the source of most reuse. These are critical people. Determine who they are and treat them well, for they will be key to the project.

10. Document the volume, velocity, and variety of content. The volume, velocity, and variety of content that crosses your desk is probably immense. Try to quantify it and use it to help justify your initiative. If nothing else, it will be an amusement to management.

11. Use business terms, not techno-babble. When talking to managers or end-users, use their terms, business terms for example, not techno-babble. This shows that you are not just a "techy" but one of them—one they may be able to trust.

12. Are you looking to implement a *point-solution* or an enterprise solution? There is a big difference between point-solutions, which serve limited users or are otherwise constrained to certain applications, and a real enterprise implementation. Don't trivialize the complexity of an enterprise solution; everything from security management to load balancing on servers to business continuity planning is required.

13. Assess an organization's technology adoption prior to system architecture. Each organization (which may be a division of a larger company) has it's own comfort level within the technology adoption cycle. Some are early adopters of new technology, while others are lagers. Determine what kind of organization you are dealing with and propose technology that is in line with their comfort level.

14. Be wary of product vendors. Their objective is to sell you their software this quarter, and they will often do whatever is necessary to make that sale. This often includes more new bugs than features, and a lack of tech support.

15. Stick with industry leading software vendors. Most of the second-, third-, and fourth-tier vendors are a notch above the guy writing code in his basement. Even the second-tier vendors usually offer very limited qualified tech support, even when they are able to make payroll that month. So stick with someone who has a truly mature product, decent market-share, and plenty of cash in the bank.

16. Get a software vendor's support plan in writing and get details. If they want your business, they will customize a document for you that outlines their proposed support for your project. It should cover telephone support, software patches, field support, and costs.

17. Don't overlook the browser incompatibility issue. As we web-enable more applications (actually, it's browser enabling) and as we add more unique plugins and use Java, the probability that all your prospective users will be able to access your new web-based application is low.

18. Manage by fact, not by emotion or your gut feelings. That also means you need facts, so ensure that the project is collecting the metrics that it should be.

19. Use Integrated Project Teams (IPTs). Your project, by its very nature, will likely involve many different type of users, making the IPT approach a necessity. This interdisciplinary team is comprised of both your staff and end-user stakeholders, working together with one single focus: project success.

20. Understand what forms of content you are dealing with, e.g. data versus information versus knowledge, and structured versus unstructured content.

21. Recognize that there is no one solution to managing content. Rather, there are a number of technologies, tools, processes, and techniques that are used to optimize content throughout the enterprise.

22. Keep all content on shared and managed servers, preferably with an Integrated Document Management (IDM) system. Do not let your employees keep content on their unmanaged local disk drives.

23. Create a comprehensive data model for your origination, complete with standard taxonomy and metadata standards.

24. Define your content retrieval needs, and utilize the appropriate tools to meet those needs; e.g. pattern matching and full-text search engines.

25. Carefully distinguish between your documents and records and establish a formal Records Management Plan, complete with retention and disposition processes and procedures.

26. Seek legal counsel's assistance when creating a Records Management Plan. Remember that many of the issues are actually legal requirements, not IT requirements.

27. Don't just focus on Word documents and your enterprise's structured database content. Remember that e-mail and voice mail files are also documents and may be subject to discovery risk.

28. Tackle preservation of content up-front with a preservation plan that includes remedies for both media disintegration and obsolescence.

29. Remember that what we are dealing with in our pursuit of Knowledge Nirvana is generally not a technical issue, but a series of issues fused by content, people, processes, and technology.

30. You already don't have any privacy and neither does your organization's content, so manage the content with the possibility of discovery in mind and articulate this concern to all employees through standardized processes and procedures.

31. Communities of Practice (CoP) exist in every organization. Recognize that fact and understand their critical role. Support them through tools and meetings that will help facilitate knowledge sharing throughout the enterprise.

32. Establish a CoP for knowledge management that covers content management and team collaboration. This will identify those who have an interest in productivity and will make your job of implementing such a system that much easier.

33. Go one step further from typical work process improvement by performing a social network analysis of how real decisions are made throughout the enterprise. Learn who really retains what knowledge.

34. We all establish content that represents "best-practices" of either the organization or our own experiences. This content, which may be a field engineer's notes, or our "cheat-sheet" of how to get something done, is often very valuable. Find it and capture this high-value content.

35. Once you deploy a portal or other content or collaboration system, the hard part starts. Maintaining the content is the downfall of most portals and repositories. Address this fact and work the operational solution into your processes.

36. Use the power of an Integrated Document Management (IDM) system. There is no excuse not to, and that is worth repeating.

37. Seek an outside consultant to perform a knowledge audit complete with a true organizational IQ assessment. Those of you in collaborative-hostile environments may find that seeking Knowledge Nirvana is just not worth it; it's best to recognize this up-front.

38. Assess the culture of collaboration in the organization. Some organizations value and reward teamwork, collaboration, and content reuse. Others do not have that culture of trust; they reward individual achievement and have many more content hoarders.

39. Provide secure dial-in access to the enterprise's content repositories and collaboration tools. This is imperative in today's global business environment characterized by knowledge-centric mobile workers.

40. Implement and support collaboration tools and related applications, such as electronic whiteboards; instant

messaging; threaded discussions; desktop and room-based video teleconferencing; shared desktops; and shared electronic workspaces.

41. Cultural issues and cultural acceptance of any new system are the greatest challenges to your success. Spend quality time understanding the organization's culture and work with the end-users; spend time with them and listen to them.

42. Pay special attention to middle management, for most of their daily activities are involved in controlling and managing content flows. Your proposed new system will likely have the greatest negative impact on middle management.

43. Focus on training and end-user support near the end of a project. Spend quality time, one-on-one, with employees; this is often all that is needed to overcome their fears.

44. We all use processes, and those processes that are repeatable and fairly structured in nature will benefit from workflow automation. Analyze your organizational processes and automate the high-value processes. This offers a quick and relatively cheap way to increase productivity.

45. Examine the sequential-oriented processes, those that have lots of "as-is" steps with long time lags between the steps. These are likely to be your high-payoff work processes that are ripe for automation.

46. Workflow applications and tools tend to come in two extremes: those that offer a lot "out of the box" and those that require significant customization and integration prior to any workflow automation. Decide which is right for you, and select your workflow solution with care.

47. If you use an ad-hoc workflow application, keep it simple. Your end-users will need to use that tool to create their own workflows, so ease of use and an intuitive interface will be key to user adoption.

48. Carefully consider any use of worker statistics that may be available from a workflow system. While there is often some interesting data on productivity, consider employee

moral and the "big-brother" consequences of tapping this data.

49. You must consider what level of process improvement you are going to undertake. All proposed systems will alter the current processes; therefore process improvement is imperative.

50. The existing, typically management-approved, processes have often evolved over time and may be radically different than what is expected. Plan on the existing approved or otherwise assumed processes to no longer be truly accurate. This is yet another reason for the process improvement phase of any project.

51. Utilize a process-modeling tool that meets your process and data modeling methodologies of choice. For example, the IDEF0 process model can be used with the simple Visio application or with more complex process automation applications. In either case, use something; it will save you countless hours of mundane box drawing.

52. Plan on hitting at least some process landmines, and manage them before they blow up and derail your project.

53. When performing process improvement, get input from as many employees as is practical; the more the better. Focus on the lowest-level employee in the organization for the most accurate information. Use management mostly for the big-picture issues and macro-level requirements.

54. Stay focused on the outcome of a process: the customer. We all have customers, and they need to be interviewed to ensure that the output of a process is actually what they want.

55. Use an electronic facilitation tool for larger groups or to promote an open discussion of requirements or processes. An electronic facilitation tool allows everyone to add their thoughts and issues without revealing who said what, all in a structured and facilitated manner.

56. Take advantage of the enterprise portal solution to provide a single interface into your disparate content repositories. Properly implemented portals will also provide a single

security sign-on which greatly improves organizational information security.

57. Lots of products are called "portals," but don't be fooled by this attempt to cast just any software product as important content and collaboration tool. A real portal must be able to search multiple repositories of both structured and unstructured content, and present the result to the user in a highly custom and personalized interface.

58. A portal project is easy to gage the success of. If users end up spending much or all of their working day in the portal, you have a success on your hands.

59. Content metadata security remains an issue with portals, especially for those organizations that rely on security classifications, such as *confidential* or *private*. Be especially careful in evaluating your prospective portal in terms of security metadata.

60. Every organization has a taxonomy. Spend time learning the taxonomy and document it. Use this baselined organizational taxonomy for further content clustering.

61. Avoid "disruptive technologies" that offer little or no perceived value to the end-user. Any new system must add real value, perceived or otherwise, in order to be judged a success by one's harshest critics—the end-user.

62. Portals need to be fed with good system administration and a healthy diet of relevant content. It is relatively easy to implement a portal. The challenge is to maintain its relevancy to the organization. If the portal does not become ubiquitous in the organization, then it will not likely receive content it needs to remain relevant.

63. There are two approaches to implementing a portal: the knowledge base and the integrated portal approach. Avoid the easier knowledge base approach, for its total cost of ownership (TCO) is much higher in the long run.

64. If you find yourself having to "remind" employees to contribute content to the portal, you have already failed.

65. While a chief sponsor, cheerleader, and project mentor is invaluable to any project, the resulting solution must be

viewed on its own as providing a true value-added service.

66. Use Knowledge Capturing Projects sparsely, for they are a last minute and desperate approach to save and categorize content. Instead, weave content capturing into all relevant processes and the overall organizational culture.

67. The physiological factor of a portal is important. Users must at all times feel that the portal is their source for enterprise content; otherwise they will revert back to other sources and methods.

68. Taxonomies change due to our ever-changing business environment. Recognize this and update your organizational taxonomy on a relatively frequent basis.

69. On the Internet, your web content is your organization, so ensure that it is perfect in every way. Have others, including legal counsel, review it for clarity.

70. You will likely end up needing to use a separate, yet integrated, web content management system (or tool) to manage your web site and it is content. Try to integrate it as closely as possible to your existing enterprise content and collaboration systems and processes.

71. For web content, separate content from the format, and separate the content creator from the template. This generally eliminates the "Web Master bottleneck" and allows you to integrate dynamic content from back-end transactional applications.

72. Assess your personal actions and project against Donald Trump's top ten list for success. Remember, think big; stay focused; be paranoid; keep your momentum going; be passionate; go against the tide; hire the best and work with the best; be lucky; have some degree of certainty; and get even (if applicable).

73. You want to reuse content, so why start from scratch on project management? Instead, seek out and use the best practices, existing methodologies, proven processes, and other valuable project management resources.

74. Think you are good? Then evaluate yourself and your project against the Software Engineering Institute's

Capability Maturity Model, run by Carnegie Mellon University. They have the best program for focusing on the maturity of business and processes to reduce risk and ensure project success.

75. Don't guess at success; measure it. Use metrics to gage the progress of a project as well as the overall outcome upon deployment. Try using a formal metrics-based objective methodology, such as the Balanced Scorecard.

76. Risk management is not just for wimps. Force yourself to follow a risk management process whereby you identify all relevant risks to the success of a project, assess their probability and impact, and establish a plan to either eliminate or decrease the effect of each risk.

77. Use the best talent available. Remember that mediocre staff usually results in mediocre outcomes. Identify the type of skills you need to ensure project success, then get them from either internal resources or by using integrators, consultants, and product vendors. Staff top down, not bottom up.

78. Communicate. There is no excuse not to. Keep an open dialog with your staff, management, and stakeholders. Manage their expectations and let them know what you expect of them at all times. Ensure full disclosure.

79. Decide early on what your acquisition plan will be. Will you outsource your project to a full-service systems integrator, or use in-house talent supported by consultants? What products will you utilize, and what support will you require from the product vendor?

80. Consider the use of an outside consultant or an IV&V contractor for any large project, regardless of your acquisition plan. Any large, complex project probably has a low probability of success anyway, so you will need all the help you can get, especially from an independent entity.

81. Make very wise software product decisions, for they will form the basis of your solution. Along with each product's fit to both your functional and technical requirements, assess the product vendor's fiscal health and their support

capabilities. Will they be around in 18 months, and if so, will they be supporting your newly purchased product?

82. Executive sponsor commitment is key to ensuring that all critical parties will work together. Commitment by the executive sponsor is much more than making a speech at the project kick-off meeting. The sponsor will need to stay involved, at a macro-level, through deployment, training, and initial support.

83. Define what business issue you will solve with your new system. Sounds simple, but it often is not. Defining the functional requirements is an art, with some people doing a much better job than others. Remember the technical requirements as well, such as what future operating system versions will need to be supported and how much bandwidth is expected to be available.

84. If network bandwidth or end-user computing resources, such as memory and disk space, are an issue, perform a system simulation. This is often the easiest way to anticipate network traffic and other resource issues. Why guess at response times when you can really anticipate them through a simulation tool?

85. Use a proven methodology, along with associated processes and procedures. Pay special attention to the strategic planning and organizational understanding needed at the beginning of any new project. This, and other key lessons learned, is fundamental to the Knowledge Nirvana methodology.

86. Utilize a content repository for all your project management needs, including process assets and general project repository content. This greatly helps in the control and reuse of every aspect of the project, and further allows your newly developed best-practices to be used throughout the enterprise.

87. Use either a waterfall or a spiral development approach, depending on the nature of the project; how well the requirements are defined; the organizations philosophy, and the competency of your staff. Either one can work

effectively; it's all a matter of fit.

88. Consider all aspects of a system deployment. For example, if you are to install in two locations, then you will inevitably have site-specific configurations and a versions control issue to overcome. With two locations, you already have three versions: your baseline development version and one for each location.

89. Users and managers expect nothing less that a 24x7 operation, not to mention instant access to enterprise content complete with personalization. So plan on the support and operations requirements. Consider a hosting center, which often offers a low-cost alternative with minimal up-front cash expenditure.

90. Provide multiple methods of training. Start with instructor-led training classes, but also rely on computer-based training (CBT), extensive on-line help, and one-on-one training.

91. Treat security as *Information Assurance*. Security is not just password management. Adopt the broader philosophy of Information Assurance, which treats all aspects of securing content throughout its life cycle.

92. Users have varied security privileges. Not everyone can and should have access to all content. Take the security requirements very seriously and ensure that your solution can adequately and easily facilitate security privileges down to a granular level; i.e., document, paragraph, record, field, etc.

93. Encourage innovation. Tacit knowledge is where innovation comes from. Encourage it within your team and from your end-users.

94. Be cool. You are implementing cool technology. Transfer this feeling to others on the team and to the users. Make them feel special, for they probably are, even if they are really a pain to deal with.

95. Have fun. Always have fun, even when you are faced with challenges from product vendors, luddites, or management.

"The first dollar I would spend
is on data integration."

— Sandy Berger,
Former National Security Advisor,
on what he would do if he were
the new Homeland Security Director.

Prologue

The Enabling Technology for Homeland Security

A s with most events throughout history, it takes the culmination of many actions leading up to a single event to bring a nation together behind a significant purpose. Today, that purpose is Homeland Security and our War on Terrorism.

Terrorism is nothing new, not even for Americans. We may have had a sense of security up until 9:05 a.m. EST on September 11, 2001, but it was only a perceived sense. The World Trade Center, after all, had been bombed before, and if it had not been such a magnificent piece of engineering, it may have previously fallen.

We have seen other terrorist attacks, primarily against the symbols of our nation abroad. In October 2000, for example, suicide bombers attacked the USS *Cole* as it refueled in the Yemen port of Aden.

America had let her guard down, right up until September 11th, now known simply as *9-11*.

We knew it was risky to refuel in Aden, but with then President Bill Clinton's meager defense budget, the U.S. Navy was forced to decommission many of its oil tankers, making risky refueling stops inevitable.

Our focus on technical intelligence gathering from land and space-born sensors grabbed the majority of funding from the classical human intelligence, known as HUMINT.

Lacking such HUMINT—real spy craft—proved fatal on 9-11, as we now know. We lacked the means to gather information on our new threat, the international terrorist organizations of al Qaeda.

We did understand their potential, we just did not know their specific actions or timing. What happened on 9-11 was not a strategic surprise. The men and woman of the intelligence community, military, public safety, and emergency response agencies had imagined such a devastating attack, including the use of airplanes as missiles. Scenarios had been developed, simulations run, and damage assessments calculated.

The thought of a terrorist willing to become a martyr in order to achieve their act is also nothing new. We have experienced it before, such as the 1983 attack against the U.S. Marine barracks in Lebanon and the attack on the USS *Cole*.

In 1998 Congress crated the *Advisory Panel to Assess Domestic Response Capabilities for Terrorism Involving Weapons of Mass Destruction*, also called the *Gilmore Commission*, chaired by former Virginia Governor James Gilmore. Effective information management and collaboration were key in their findings, which produced specific recommendations, such as the need to create a single *Boarder Security Awareness* repository.

Having served for the U.S. Intelligence Community, and having built intelligence collaboration systems, I understand the real challenges of implementing a useful information sharing solution. As with any content and collaboration system, whether deployed for Shell Oil or for the CIA, the challenges are often not technical. Rather, they are organizational, procedural, and process-based; the *human factors* issues of knowledge management.

Interagency turf wars have made sharing and collaboration a near impossibility. Today, there is little real sharing of meaningful content between any of the Homeland Security-related organizations. Worse yet, the idea of sharing such content with state officials has traditionally been brushed off as something that will simply never happen.

While turf wars and other cultural issues are the primary impediment, there do exist some unique challenges related to intelligence.

The classification of content is often a major inhibitor to sharing and the subsequent collaboration between members of a community of practice. Indirectly revealing one's sources and methods of intelligence collection is a very valid concern raised anytime you share content or fuse all-source intelligence from many sources. Even international treaties and memoranda of understanding between governments often severely restrict the use of content provided by that foreign intelligence service.

While all this can be overcome, they nevertheless add yet another layer of complexity on top of the already complicated cultural and turf war issues encountered on any knowledge management initiative.

Many agencies within the Federal Government, exemplified by the Intelligence Community, have pockets of impressive technology use. There exists, however, a real disparity between agencies and even between the many programs within each agency.

The widest technology chasm has traditionally been with the many law enforcement, public safety, and criminal justice organizations of the Federal Government. Having built systems for these organizations over the years, I witnessed first-hand their lack of adequate IT infrastructure and mission-specific applications, and I am not alone in this obvious realization. U.S. Attorney General John Ashcroft, testifying before Congress, recently stated, "We must have information technology from this decade, not several generations ago, so we can share intelligence." Ashcroft defined three new focus areas: information sharing; information analysis; and coordination. Applying the principals found in this book would go a long way towards meeting those three challenges.

Efficient content and collaboration systems rely on a sound infrastructure complete with reasonable computers, servers, and communications. There are those in the FBI who still don't have general e-mail access. For a long time, the more progressive Special Agents resorted to using America Online (AOL), which was affectionately dubbed the *FBI's E-mail System*. There still is no enterprise records management system in use at the FBI today. This is evident by the last-minute discovery of thousands of missing documents related to the trial of Oklahoma City bomber Timothy

McVeigh. At best, this was just a terrible embarrassment for the Bureau, having made the front page of most every paper in America. At worst, it is a symptom of an organization that has little in the way of enterprise systems and applications to manage their most valuable asset—information content.

This occurs at the same time that it has been widely reported (but not confirmed) that Osama bin Laden's al Qaeda organization had been communicating throughout Europe by encrypting their text and hiding it in graphics images published on the Internet in plain site. This covert means of communications, called stenography, is advanced technically and is very difficult to detect.

Fortunately, long-delayed improvements in IT capability for the FBI and other agencies are now planned. The various Homeland Security legislative bills have finally provided ample IT funding for organizations such as the FBI. There are signs of hope within Federal law enforcement, for they, too, have pockets of successful IT systems. The FBI's Integrated Automated Fingerprint Identification System (IAFIS), built by Litton PRC (now part of Northrop Grumman) and Lockheed Martin, has revolutionized fingerprint matching and has taken violent criminals off the street. Systems such as IAFIS prove that, with adequate funding, the right leadership, and the technical competence of both in-house and contracted support, IT can make a difference for America.

知

Our sense of security as a nation was shattered on the tragic morning of 9-11. Turning commercial jetliners into missiles was a horrendous act, as terrorists plowed these airplanes into the World Trade Center towers and the Pentagon, killing more than 3,000 innocent civilians. A forth jetliner went down in Pennsylvania, thanks to the bravery of the passengers on board. That plane was believed to be headed for the White House or the Capitol building in Washington, D.C.

As we watched the events of that day unfold live on television, many of us asked ourselves and our coworkers how such a thing could happen. Could it have been prevented? How did those terrorists manage to carry out such a coordinated attack that certainly took extensive planning and funding? Could we have known what they were attempting to do and could we have stopped it?

There are those who have labeled the events leading up to 9-11 as an information failure. That label is hard to dispute, given what we now know.

We know that many sources in law enforcement, the U.S. Department of Justice, and the Intelligence Community knew a great deal about the hijackers and their accomplices prior to the attacks. What they lacked, however, was an enterprise management capability to effectively manage the content (data and information) and the collaboration needed to adequately assess that content. In that respect, it was clearly an information failure.

Granted, not enough was likely known to have foiled the attacks of that day, but it is still troubling how much was known. One man, Youssef Hmimssa, apparently entered and left the country illegally, almost at will. He was even captured, not once but twice, only to be released because of faulty, misleading, and untimely data.

Other terrorists were known and were on various "watch lists," which are comprised of basic structured data. All 19 of the 9-11 terrorists had obtained social security cards, and 13 of them did so legally, according to James Huse, Jr., the Social Security Administration's Inspector General, during testimony before Congress a month after the attack.

Some of the structured data residing in those watch lists is shared between various government agencies, but most of it is not. It is also fairly easy to fool a watch list—just misspell a name or use aliases. Most of the data we have concerning potential terrorists resides in the same content containers that house most corporate content; e.g., documents, paper forms, and e-mail. Today, not one of the major Federal law enforcement agencies has a substantive automated case management system. Case management is a vertical knowledge management application that combines the unstructured content containers with structured data, such as those on watch lists. The use of workflow and other collaboration tools greatly enhances the case management application, which is currently used in only a limited manner.

Today, the Government does not have the ability to construct a collective view of the terrorists. Instead, content relating to each of the 19 terrorists exists in literally hundreds of databases that, for the most part, are not integrated in even the simplest manner. Other key content exists in paper forms and documented reports that usually sit in paper case folders, no different than they did when the FBI was chasing Bonnie and Clyde in the 1930's. The INS still has not automated their most basic files on alien residents and visitors, know as *AFILES*, thus ensuring that those aliens who wish to do us harm have the upper hand when they are among us.

The commercial sector recently experienced a similar problem of disparate content concerning their customers. To solve that problem, industry created a new class of applications called Customer Relationship Management (CRM) systems. These are repositories and portals that allow authorized employees to view all relevant content pertaining to a customer in an organized and efficient context. What the Government needs today is to start acting like a modern knowledge enterprise, complete with the *single view of the terrorist.*

Creating the single view of the terrorist is remarkably similar to the issues that have already been overcome by knowledge management practitioners, which entails managing content; people; processes; and technology.

Fortunately, many leading politicians and Government IT managers have recognized the value of effectively managing content and improving collaboration, and are now actively promoting knowledge management as a key technology for enabling Homeland Security. Managing content, collaboration, and processes will enable the real-time decision-making necessary in today's post 9-11 environment.

Knowledge management has been pushed to the forefront of the War on Terrorism by automating the *situational awareness* capability of the enterprise. This includes supporting threat assessments, counter terrorism activities, threat reduction, threat response, and disaster recovery. Knowledge Management is key to supporting all of these, due to its ability to offer four key functional capabilities necessary for Homeland Security. These are:

- Trigger Events—Imagine a foreign student who changes their doctoral major from home economics to molecular biology. In today's post 9-11 society, that change is an event that should trigger an action or notification. While the Government currently uses some trigger events, there is still no adequate means for managing those events throughout the enterprise. A Knowledge Management system for the enterprise would provide the foundation necessary to manage these events in an effective manner.
- Patterns of Conduct—Someone just purchased an anthrax technical journal and visited a crop-dusting web site. What do you do? Knowledge Management provides the ability to both detect that pattern of conduct and to manage the response. Like trigger events, managing the pattern of conduct is about managing content in a controlled, secure, and collaborative manner.
- Collaboration—Efficiently collaborating content is paramount to unraveling complex terrorist activities. With over 40 Federal offices and agencies directly supporting Homeland Security, the need to efficiently collaborate between them is unmistakable. Knowledge Management offers the only cost effective solution for this form of secure collaboration.
- Business Continuity—A side benefit to an automated Knowledge Management system is the ability to quickly backup or otherwise distribute content. For example, case folders existed in a CIA office located in the World Trade Center. With a content management solution, those folders would not have been lost in the building's collapse, as was widely published in the news media. Instead, the system would have allowed the content to be automatically co-located to a second facility in near real-time. An automated content solution acts as a contingency plan, ensuring that no catastrophic loss will destroy an enterprise's content.

The Government faces unique challenges that greatly complicate effective knowledge sharing. Former CIA Director James Woolsey, commenting to me on the Government's difficulty in sharing knowledge, stated that, "Not everyone in (the U.S.) Government is necessarily on our side; and I refer to Robert Hanson" (the FBI mole who worked for the KGB).

While most commercial companies are merely worried about protecting a customer's credit card number, the Government must carefully protect the secrecy of millions of content assets. Effective sharing of these assets must include an enterprise-wide security architecture that includes business rules that define who is authorized access and who has a *need to know*.

Although the Government has those unique challenges, not one of them is insurmountable. What you have learned in this book is how to implement successful Knowledge Management solutions necessary to achieve the competitive advantage. Significant improvements are attainable whether you are implementing a collaboration system for General Electric or a counter-terrorism portal for the CIA.

Hopefully those responsible for protecting our homeland will continue to promote the need for Knowledge Management and will utilize the guidance and lessons learned in this book to ensure that the tragic events of September 11, 2001 never occur again.

December 11, 2001
Washington, D.C.

"There are three
difficulties in authorship:

—to write anything worth publishing
—to find honest men to publish it
—and to get sensible men to read it."

– Caleb C. Colton (1780-1832)
English clergyman

About the Author

J üris Kelley is a leading developer and consultant of information technology solutions designed to accelerate an organization's cycle of innovation. He focuses on content management and optimizing team collaboration to achieve the organizational competitive advantage. Mr. Kelley has consulted leading public sector organizations and Fortune 100 companies, and has held project- through executive-level positions in virtually every aspect of the information technology life-cycle. He has also performed intermittent bouts of management and marketing, which he attributes to El Niño. During the past 15 years he has designed, developed, and installed numerous systems, ranging from small departmental applications to several international solutions, each serving over 20,000 users. Mr. Kelley is a technology mentor with the University of Maryland's Smith School of Business and serves on the ANSI C.22 standards committee for electronic content legality. He resides in Reston, Virginia.

"The best part of our knowledge
is that which teaches us
where knowledge leaves off
and ignorance begins."

– Oliver Wendell Holmes (1809-1894)
American poet and author

Glossary

Ad Hoc Workflow—An unstructured relatively simple work process that is often created on the spot as required by the end-user; simple routing and forwarding functionality

Alphanumeric—Field type that contains both characters and numbers

AOL—America Online

ASCII—American Standard Code for Information Interchange; the typical character set used today for computer characters

As-Is Model—Representation of the current state; usually a process model that depicts the current or existing processes; opposite of the to-be model

Balanced Scorecard—Formal metrics-based project evaluation methodology commonly used to justify IT projects

Best Practices—Documented processes and standards that have been found to work exceptionally well in the past; optimized processes

BPR—Business Process Reengineering; a radical approach to process improvement characterized by starting over with all new processes

Business Continuity—The ability to maintain business operations during or after a contingency or related catastrophe

Business Rule—Logical condition or rule that is often a functional input used during system development

Business Intelligence Systems—see Decision Support Systems

CKO—Chief Knowledge Officer; the senior manager responsible for content and collaboration initiatives throughout an organization

CMM—Capability Maturity Model; a five level rating method used to assess the business and process maturity of an organization or project

Collaboration—The act of working together for a common objective; employees or others who work together

Community of Interest—see Community of Practice

Community of Practice—Coalition of employees who share a similar interest or work process

Compound Document—Any document that contains multiple data types or formats

Consumer Portal—A semi-personalized search and retrieval application often used for the Internet

Content—The subject matter of a document; data and information

Content Creator—Author; characterized by one who creates text that is usually distinct from the formatting of the eventual document

Content Repository—Any storage system of data, information, or pre-defined processes

Context—Relationship of a document or content container to other related documents, actions, or authors

Cookies—Semi-temporary files stored on a computer by a web application that assists in determining who you are and your preferences

CRM—Customer Relationship Management; general term for a class of applications that manage customer information and related transactions

Customization—The ability to tailor a system or application to meet one's requirements

Data—Basic unrefined and generally unfiltered content

Database—Computer file/system that is optimized to manage structured data

Decision Support Systems—Aggregates large quantities of structured data to drive automated analysis and provide decision options to management

Desktop Video Teleconferencing—see Video Teleconferencing

Discovery—The legal process by which attorneys discover what records or other content exist

Disintegration (of media)—The destruction of the physical aspects of media; e.g., CD-ROMs and floppy disks

Disruptive Technology—System, application, or technology that is perceived as offering little or no value to the end-user and is, therefore, disruptive to one's daily work

Document—Any container of data or information that has content, context, and structure

Document Management System—Application that manages documents such as Word, Excel, and PowerPoint; may also manage processes and document images

Dynamic Content—Data or information that is rendered in real-time usually from a back-end transactional-based applications

Early Adopters—Organizations or individuals that utilize technology, specific products, or product versions prior to their general use in their respective industry

Electronic Whiteboard—Computer monitor-based collaboration application allowing multiple individuals to share the content of a single virtual whiteboard often used for brainstorming

Enterprise Document Management System—see Integrated Document Management

Enterprise Portal—see Portal

ERP—Enterprise Resource Planning; general class of applications that manage back-office organizational content, such as employee or financial data

Executive Sponsor—Senior-level manager of the end-user organization that is the official supporter of a project

Groupware—Semi-structured discussions from communities of practices; a class of collaboration applications

Hit-list—The return of a search finding

HTML—HyperText Markup Language; the typical file formatting used by the Internet documents

Human Factors—Reference to the multitude of issues regarding a human's use of any automated system

HUMINT—Human Intelligence; the collection of intelligence from non-technical means

IAFIS—Integrated Automated Fingerprint Identification System

IDEF—Integrated DEFinition; a process and data modeling standard

Imaging System—An IT system designed to manage scanned documents; the pre-cursor to Integrated Document Management

Infoglut—An overload of content

Information—Data that has evolved to the point of being useful for analysis or summarization

Instant Messaging—Application or tool that allows multiple individuals to virtually chat with one another on a single computer monitor

Integrated Document Management—Comprehensive content management system for managing multiple content types, such as structured documents and TIFF image files; often includes processes and web content management

Integrated Repository—One of two general portal approaches that integrates the content of multiple repositories into a single portal

Integrator—An IT firm that combines various systems, tools, and applications to create an integrated solution for solving business requirements

IP—Internet Protocol

IT—Information Technology

IV&V—Independent Verification and Validation; an IT firm or consultant that reviews the work and schedule of others, usually of a systems integrator or developer

Jump-start Kit—Self-contained package of resources used to accelerate a new project, often containing best practices, documentation, tools, guidance, and lessons learned

Killer-app—Application that is transforming in nature

Knowledge—The tacit content within our minds derived by awareness and comprehension of one's experiences

Knowledge Audit—Analysis of an organization's knowledge and content, how it flows, and what obstacles to collaboration may exist

Knowledge Base—Single repository containing content that has been imported from their original repositories; one of two portal approaches

Knowledge Capture—Process or project whereby "knowledge engineers" save and categorize content from subject matter experts

Knowledge Engineer—Individual who performs knowledge capture tasks or related content initiatives

Knowledge Harvesting—Actively capturing and cataloging content from a knowledge worker; may include videotaping a knowledge worker

Knowledge Management—Concept that combines content with organizational processes and people, as well as the technologies that enable their effective use

Knowledge Nirvana—Methodology for use in content and collaboration projects or related initiatives

Knowledge Worker—General term referring to white-collar employees who utilize their tacit knowledge along with organizational content to make decisions

Legacy Application—System or application that currently exists in an organization that is usually not of the same architecture of a newly implemented or proposed system; an old system or application

Metadata—Data about data, such as a field name, description, and type

Methodology—Defined and structured process for performing a task or project, comprised of an overall strategy and individual process

Migration Plan—Content preservation plan for transferring content onto newer formats, applications, operating systems, and hardware; plan for transferring or importing content from one application to another

NARA—National Archives and Records Administration; the Federal agency responsible for records management and issuing records regulations, guidance, and procedures

Obsolescence—The irrelevancy of file formats, computer applications, operating systems, hardware, or content over time

Organizational IQ—The level of an organization's maturity of content sharing, repeatable processes, and knowledge management

PDF—Portable Document Format; a popular document format from Adobe

Personalization—The ability to adapt an application to your individual tastes and requirements; often in terms of content delivery, screen color, and font size

PIM—Personal Information Manager; application that manages personal information, such as phone numbers and appointments

Portal—Application that provides a single interface into multiple content repositories, offering a single query capability and returning a single hit list

Pull (information)—Content retrieval mode characterized by the user overtly requesting the content by query and retrieving; the opposite of information push

Push (information)—Content retrieval mode characterized by an automated system providing content to a user without their directly requesting the content; the opposite of information pull

Precision—Documents returned in a search that are relevant, usually defined as a percentage

Preservation—The act of managing the disintegration and obsolescence of content and all required components needed to retrieve and utilize the content

Process—Series of actions or functions performed to complete an operation

Process Automation—Computerization of a work process that is likely manual in nature, often automated by the use of a workflow application or tool

Process Improvement—The act of improving the process of an organization usually in a formal manner; also see BPR

Process Map—Diagram of a process showing individual steps; may be either an as-is or to-be model

Production Workflow—Structured, often defined and repeatable work process that is automated

Recall—Measure of the documents accurately identified from a repository, usually defined as a percentage

Record—Document or other content container that is a recording of an action or decision that serves as evidence of the transaction, decision, or action

Records Management—The act of managing, preserving, and destroying formal or otherwise controlled content

Records Management System—An Integrated Document Management system that also includes records retention and disposition functionality

ROI—Return on Investment

Risk Mitigation—Plan for formally identifying and managing project risk

Schedule—The act of determining which document is a record

Shared Desktop—Application or tool that allows multiple distant individuals to share a single desktop; used by computer technicians to take control of a distant desktop

Shared Workspace—Shared application used for collaboration; may be a shared repository or a document markup application

Single Sign-on—The ability to login and authenticate oneself only once, whereby an automated system manages all other logins with relevant systems or applications

Situational Awareness—Being overtly aware of a specific state, condition, or status

SME—Subject Matter Expert; a technical or functional expert

Social Network Analysis—The analysis of how a group or organization informally communicates or makes decisions

Spidering—Scanning a web-based repository to create an index

Stakeholder—Any individual who has an interest in an activity or system; often end-users, management, etc.

Stop Words—Common words such as "a" and "the" that are often omitted during indexing due to their irrelevancy

Stovepipe—System or application that offers a limited number of functions or supports a limited number of users; generally is not enterprise in its architecture

Structure (of a document)—The general document type

Structured Content—Data and information that is of a fixed length and type; usually managed in databases

Structured Databases—see Database

Supply Chain—The entire cycle or process of a system or related application

Tacit Knowledge—A person's institutional knowledge gained through experience; knowledge that exists between one's ears

Taxonomy—Organized hierarchy of subjects or names used to assist content categorization

Team—Generally a defined work group organized to solve a specific objective

Technology Laggards—Organizations or individuals that trail others in the general use of technology, products, or versions of products

Technology Refresh—Utilizing new technology in an existing system or application; the cycle-time of utilizing newer technology

Template—A formatting outline or structure for the insertion of content

Threaded Discussion—Topic-based dialogue whereby multiple individuals append their comments onto an existing discussion

TIFF—Tagged Image File Format; the standard format for scanned documents

TIFF Header—Semi-structured metadata repository of a TIFF file

To-Be Model—A formal representation depicting the future or proposed state of a process; opposite of the as-is model

Unstructured Content—Data and information that is not of fixed length and type, such as a Word document or a graphics file

Version Control—A tool or application that manages the versions of content or a document, usually with data/time and author data

Video Teleconferencing—Video and audio-based conferencing system allowing distant individuals to virtually collaborate in a joint meeting

Visio—A simple diagramming application made by Microsoft

Web Content Management—Application designed to manage the life cycle of web content creation and usage, typically for Internet or Intranet content

Watch List—Any list of individuals who are suspected of illegal activity; an automated database of suspects

Web Master—One who manages a web site

Workflow—Application or tool designed to automate work processes or similar tasks

WYSIWYG—What You See Is What You Get

XML—eXtensible Markup Language; a web-based text and formatting protocol that provides more control than HTML

"My dear fellow,
there can be no sort of achievement,
without some kind of ordeal."

—*From the play The Imaginary Invalid*
By Miles Malleson (1622-1673)

Index

CPSIA information can be obtained at www.ICGtesting.com
Printed in the USA
LVOW080147270412

279243LV00004B/119/A